Alice
and the Machine Gunner

Alice, emigrant, survivor, matriarch and time traveller.

Alice
and the Machine Gunner

David J. Forsyth

Rock's Mills Press
Oakville, Ontario
2022

AUTHOR'S NOTE

While the spelling of Alice's surname varied with each generation, its earliest known version has been maintained throughout the narrative to avoid confusion.

Published by
Rock's Mills Press
www.rocksmillspress.com

Copyright © 2022 by David J. Forsyth.
All rights reserved.

For information about this book, including retail, wholesale and bulk orders, contact the publisher at customer.service@rocksmillspress.com.

*This book is dedicated
to "Queen"
who spent her life accumulating
the memories that she entrusted to me.*

*. . . and Jack,
with whom I will always associate
the word "hero"*

The past is ever present,
for though my great-grandfathers languish
in forgotten graves,
the character of my life
is the product of their existence.

CONTENTS

PREFACE xi

INTRODUCTION xiii

CHAPTER ONE
THE GEHERTYS OF CASTLEPOLLARD 3

CHAPTER TWO
THOMAS'S BURDEN 11

CHAPTER THREE
STEAM PACKETS AND STAGE COACHES 21

CHAPTER FOUR
THE IMMIGRANT 31

CHAPTER FIVE
A CHILD OF ST. LUKE'S 41

CHAPTER SIX
CHANGE OF FORTUNE 49

CHAPTER SEVEN
A GIFT OF STRAWBERRIES 57

CHAPTER EIGHT
JOSEPH'S THIRD SON 67

CHAPTER NINE
THE COMING TOGETHER 79

CHAPTER TEN
DISTANT THUNDER 91

CHAPTER ELEVEN
FRENCH MUD AND MUSTARD GAS 99

CHAPTER TWELVE
A WOMAN'S VOICE 109

CHAPTER THIRTEEN
ALICE'S SECRET   119

CHAPTER FOURTEEN
BELGIUM BOUND   127

CHAPTER FIFTEEN
TEN DAYS AT SEA   139

CHAPTER SIXTEEN
THE DEPRESSION   149

CHAPTER SEVENTEEN
SECOND WIND   161

CHAPTER EIGHTEEN
ALICE'S HERO   169

CHAPTER NINETEEN
THE GOOD YEARS   183

CHAPTER TWENTY
ASHES TO ASHES   191

PREFACE

When we peer into the past, we encounter shadows somewhere around our fifth birthday. For most of us, that's where our earliest memories reside. At that point, the shadows thicken and become impenetrable. Everything beyond them is history, the interpretation of which relies on those who have preceded us. Academic history shines its selective spotlight on significant events, but its glare tends to obscure the histories of millions of ordinary people. Aside from a handful of memories entrusted to friends and family, their stories are forever lost.

Because we're unable to see beyond our own recollections, we tend to forget that reality continues into the darkness, where our grandparents, and *their* grandparents, once experienced a world far different from ours. My purpose is simply to illuminate the darkness. For me, writing *Alice and the Machine Gunner* was about turning on the light to enable *this* generation to see beyond the shadows, into the day-to-day lives of our ancestors.

Alice, and the generations that created her, witnessed and contributed to history as surely as kings and queens and seafaring explorers. They too must be illuminated, if only to acknowledge their daily struggle for survival. Alice's story echoes the ancestral tales of many families by describing how she came to be, how she found love, and how for the sake of that love, she found the courage to abandon everything familiar and dear.

By generously sharing her stories at the kitchen table over many years, Alice, in effect, co-authored this book. Her black-and-white photographs, hoarded correspondence, and the public record filled in many of the remaining gaps. The resulting material, though lacking too many details to be described as a biography, is more than sufficient to compile an 'almost' true story of her and her ancestors.

While Alice and her life experience warrant a full-fledged biography, I have to accept that no one remains to provide the details of much of her life. I therefore offer this account of her and her ancestors as a work of creative non-fiction based on the information which has survived.

David J. Forsyth

INTRODUCTION

At the western tip of Canada's Lake Ontario, in the industrial city of Hamilton, a cemetery called White Chapel Memorial Gardens passively welcomes successive generations. There, imbedded in the sod and spattered on sunny afternoons with the lacy shadows of an overhanging maple tree, lies a weathered grave marker. It is, as I write, slightly tilted, scarred by the slashing blade of a transient lawn mower, and partially covered by wind-blown snow. The word "Alice" stands in relief above its cold, hard surface. Those five bronze letters, abandoned to the frost and all but lost to the past, are the inspiration for the story that awaits the reader.

Though Alice's life barely dipped its toes into the late Victorian Era, her story wades boldly through the entire nineteenth century, where only vaguely aware of their contributions, her parents, grandparents and great-grandparents began writing her narrative. Their genes and values shaped her, and through her, influenced the lives of her descendants. Their religious, social, and economic struggles interlock like jigsaw pieces to make up Alice's story. Her cultural roots, while firmly anchored in Ireland's County Westmeath, became inexorably entwined with English beliefs, perceptions and behaviours. As a result, this book does not begin with Alice's birth in 1898, but rather among the hopes and dreams of previous generations, both Irish and English.

The book is based on actual events and real people, and is as close to truth as is possible whilst relying exclusively on yellowed documents, family anecdotes, and years of historical research.

The writer has employed fiction only where reality has been lost to the passage of time. In some cases, hours of study preceded the composition of a few paragraphs in an effort to reconstruct an historically accurate and plausible account of forgotten events. Still, every effort has been made to adhere to the known facts and the most likely scenarios. Ideally the reader will embrace the Gehertys' story as a whole and not focus excessively on what must obviously be fictitious dialogue.

Alice was an exceptional individual and an inspiration to all who knew her. She impacted countless lives over the better party of a century through her understanding, integrity, gentleness, and perseverance. She accepted the role assigned her by the culture of her time and fulfilled it dutifully. She was 'Jack's wife' and proud to be so. Her aspirations were for those she loved. She quietly put the needs of her spouse and children before her own, yet every decision that she made was *hers*. Alice was strong, wise, and more in control of her destiny than those around her understood.

The book begins in the ancient village of Castlepollard, Ireland where Alice's grandfather, Thomas, was raised by a linen weaver and his wife. It chronicles the young man's emigration to England at the beginning of The Great Famine and his life in London's Parish of St. Luke, Old Street. The focus of the narrative turns to Thomas's son, Peter, who grows up motherless amid prejudice and poverty and finds his way to a better life. When Peter's young wife gives birth to their first child, she is baptised Alice Rose, but her father nicknames her *Queen*. Peter's only daughter, on the cusp of womanhood when the Great War begins, falls in love with a soldier from Canada and is forced to choose between her family and a man destined to return to his home across the Atlantic. When RMS *Corsican* sails out of the port of Liverpool in August of 1919, the reality of never seeing her mum and dad again is overwhelming, as it must have been for approximately 35,000 British women in the wake of World War One. Alice's story is shared by thousands of Canadian families which count British war-brides among their ancestors.

Much of the narrative you are about to read was composed through watery eyes, a reflection of my profound love and respect for a woman who deserves to be remembered long after *I* have ceased to exist.

Alice
and the Machine Gunner

CHAPTER ONE

THE GEHERTYS OF CASTLEPOLLARD

More often than not, she called me *Ducky*, a remnant of the 1919 world she abandoned beyond the salty swells of the North Atlantic. The affectionate term was a reflection of her love for me. Wrapped in the pink and green floral pattern of a bibbed apron, she moved easily between the oven and the love-worn kitchen table. The room was her domain, her refuge from those events that were beyond her control. Her life experience was her strength; it steeled her against the world. In her presence, I felt only warmth, security and peace. She was my mother's mother, and I called her Nana. Her given name was Alice.

Alice understood tears – hers and ours. She generously and unconditionally shared her love, her values, and her acquired wisdom. Those who sought her counsel received it without judgement. She was at peace with the world because she had, long ago, forgiven it. Relinquishing her tenacious grip on life in the autumn of 1988, Alice slipped gently into the memories of those she had touched.

Alice's life was more than half over by the time I was born. Another Alice, one who had preceded the wise matriarch I called Nana, had once known the innocence of adolescence and felt the self-consciousness of a teenager. She had experienced love and the insecurities of a young bride about to embark on a new life far from everything familiar to her. Exiled from family and the beloved city of her youth, she struggled to adjust while her family and her responsibilities grew; all that before I was born.

Alice's story began with a tentative effort to exhume her past based on trivial accounts of events, places, people and times. She had related them to me over many years while we sat drinking tea at her kitchen table. Her tales were offered casually and without pretence; each story, a souvenir of enormous value, a snippet of her past.

As I listened, I often envied her ability to see the places and the people of whom she spoke. After her death, I resolved to preserve those memories;

those personal flash-backs that meant so much to her, and which future generations might view as history. So, I began.

I tried in earnest to reconstruct and comprehend, as best I could, how Alice had experienced life over nine decades. My research began with a record of her birth. There, on the certificate, were the details of her parents. I immediately recognized that while the moment of her birth was in fact a beginning, there were other beginnings before her birth and still others, receding indistinctly into her forgotten lineage.

Alice's story of innocence, passion, adventure and endurance extends back, beyond her ninety years of her life, into the shadowy antiquity of early nineteenth-century Ireland. Today, it touches seven generations and embraces two continents.

So, I began again.

∞∞∞∞∞∞∞∞∞∞∞∞∞∞∞∞∞∞∞∞∞∞∞∞∞∞∞∞∞∞∞∞∞∞

Few details escaped the grey-green mists of a time when, in Westmeath, Ireland, the pall of Protestant ascendancy and Roman Catholic subjugation lingered in the shadow of Castlepollard's St. Michael's Church. The indifferent passage of the years has eroded written accounts and erased innumerable memories that once lived in the first decade of the nineteenth century. Still, it is a certainty that those then native to Ireland, including Alice's ancestors, shared the blood of the enigmatic Celts who flourished throughout central and northern Europe long before the more celebrated Roman period.

The Celtic tribes of Ireland had a rich and prosperous cultural heritage of literature, law, medicine, economics, industry and warfare. The Irish language, based on the twenty-character Ogham alphabet, is the third-oldest literary language in Europe, predated only by Greek and Latin. The origins of the Celtic legal system, the Brehon Laws, date to the eighth century B.C. Two centuries later, the Celts were making glass, using it primarily in the production of jewellery and ornamental representations of animals. They minted their own distinctive coinage prior to the late fourth century B.C., some fifty years *before* Roman coins appeared. The Bronze helmets of their warriors, topped with elaborate projections and fitted with cheek guards, were only later adopted by the Romans along with facsimiles of Celtic shields. Europe's first known hospital, Bróin Bherg (house of sorrow), was established in 377 B.C. at Emain Macha in Armagh.

This fascinating history of Celtic cultural innovation had already been abrogated by centuries of foreign subjugation by the time Peter Geherty was born at Castlepollard about 1897.

Peter Geherty, a name recorded beneath "Father's Name and Surname" on an 1846 certificate of marriage, marks the beginning of Alice's story. Peter was her great-grandfather, and though her precise recall of birthdates and wedding anniversaries included aunts and uncles, cousins and grandparents, she knew nothing of Peter, despite the fact that her own father had been named in his honour. Nevertheless, Alice's great-grandfather was her tenuous link to Ireland; he was her forgotten beginning.

Until the mid-twelfth century, the predominantly agricultural population of Ireland enjoyed joint ownership of the land under locally elected chiefs. Then Ireland changed dramatically and forever, when one such leader invited Norman mercenaries to support him in a dispute with neighbouring communities. The foreign warriors eagerly seized the lands of defeated chiefs. Thereafter, each time that Irish discontent erupted into rebellion, additional warriors poured in from England to uphold the status quo. Assimilation of the Irish into the conquerors' culture was thwarted when England, under King Henry VIII, rejected Papal authority and established the Church of England. The Roman Catholic natives of the Emerald Isle were no longer bound together solely by economic oppression. Over the next three hundred years, their religious convictions sustained them in their collective struggle against foreign, anti-Papal oppression.

In 1597, an English Army captain from Devonshire, named Nicholas Pollard, arrived in Ireland to participate in a conflict with Irish forces. Subsequent to his successful campaign, Queen Elizabeth awarded Pollard a grant of land in Kinturk, a fertile Westmeath valley nurtured by nearby lakes. There, Pollard built a fortified manor which became known as Castle Pollard. His seventeenth-century descendants prospered and founded the village of Castlepollard at the junction of five roads. Those roads, like the spokes of a wheel, converged on an open space where each year, on the twenty-first day of May, the annual town fair was held. By the early nineteenth century, the tiny community had grown to include 280 houses. It is from this tiny Irish hamlet that the first murmurs of Alice's ancestors emerge.

Ireland's English occupiers introduced laws forbidding the education of Catholics and excluding them from public office. Nor were they permitted to vote, purchase land, practice law or openly attend Catholic services. Many Roman Catholic Priests, viewed as community leaders and instigators of opposition, fled to Europe of their own accord. Those who didn't were forcibly exiled or executed. By the middle of the seventeenth century, a third of Ireland's Roman Catholic population had been slaughtered, and three quarters of its farmland was in the hands of Protestant invaders. Protestant influence dominated the religiously saturated lives of everyone under England's control.

Those in the tenacious grip of Catholicism endured poverty and degradation at the hands of their Protestant overseers. While the treatment of Ireland's Catholics was abhorrent, it's difficult to fault the passion of either religious view at the time because the indoctrination of generations locked both congregations into rigid structures of conformity. Independent thinking and dissension were incomprehensible to members of both religions.

It was in the context of these events that Alice's Irish-Catholic ancestors suffered inescapable oppression from birth to death. Additional hardships, misfortunes that haunted Catholics and Protestants alike, compounded their early-nineteenth-century struggle for survival. Infant mortality, plague, and even the climate challenged families on both sides of the Irish Sea. Their frail lives, inexorably balanced on the sharp edge of fortune, might suddenly be tipped in either direction without warning.

When Peter was a young man of nineteen or twenty years, much of Europe barely survived a food shortage of unprecedented brutality. Nothing grew that summer, and neither he, nor any of his fellow countrymen had the slightest understanding of what had triggered the bizarrely cold weather. It was simply accepted as *God's will.*

More than a year earlier, in April of 1815, the most powerful volcano of the last 10,000 years began to erupt. For three months, Java's Mount Tambora vigorously and continuously expelled lava and hot embers into the Southeast Asian sky. It saturated the upper atmosphere with ash, reflecting an estimated fifth of the sun's radiation back into space. Weather throughout the world was so much affected that 1816 became known among Europeans as *the year without a summer.*

Westmeath's nineteenth century weather wasn't always cold and wet. In 1823, the year that Peter's eldest son, Thomas, was baptised, millions of five-petal flax blooms scented the mid-August air, painting the fields

Irish thatched cottage (photo by Jaclyn E. Grant).

around Castle Pollard blue. Then, within days, the idyllic countryside was overwhelmed with the stench of decomposing plants, steeping in shallow ponds just beyond the town's boundaries. The process of transforming flax into linen was an ancient and complex cycle that began each April, with the sowing of seeds from the previous year's harvest. Then in August, the blue-blossomed, metre-high plants were gently pulled by hand from the soft Irish soil and bundled into *beets*, to be carted to nearby fallow fields. There, the crofters' wives and daughters stacked them into stooks to dry in the sun prior to a process known as *retting*. This step involved the relocation of the beets to shallow ponds or ditches known as retting damns where they were left to steep for about ten days. The laborious task of recovering the stinking, sodden plants from the water was left to the men. Throughout the process, a pungent odour enveloped them and invaded every street and laneway of nearby Castlepollard. In spite of the unpleasant fumes, the process was tolerated because it promoted the separation of the stem fibres. In early September, the plants were again dried in nearby fields at the pleasure of the fickle Irish summer. By beating the dried stems vigorously with wooden paddles or mallets, a process known as *scrutching*, flax farmers produced tangled bunches of fibres. Only after they were combed straight could the spinning and weaving of linen cloth begin.

A hand-written parish record reveals that Peter Geherty married Mary Hannon at Castlepollard on 16 October 1818. One of hundreds of Westmeath linen weavers, Peter shared a humble stone cottage alongside the Mullingar Road with his wife, their children and a well-worn, hand-operated loom. Never more than a meal away from hunger, though better off than many of their neighbours, the family endured as had countless generations of Gehertys before them.

Mary Hannon Geherty dedicated much of her life to spinning flax fibres into yarn under less-than-ideal conditions. Even at mid-day, the interior of the thatched, stone cottage was often cold and always dark. A single tiny window was the only source of natural light. On most days, the weaver's wife left the rough-hewn wooden door ajar to admit a little more light. During the evenings, when the smoky flame of a tallow candle flickered erratically beneath the soot encrusted thatch, she squinted and leaned instinctively closer to her work. The rhythmic rocking of Mary's foot on the treadle and the repetitive squeak of the wheel, like the insidious onset of arthritis in the joints of her fingers, went unnoticed.

With each passing year, Peter turned crops of flax into linen cloth with the help of his wife and fathered children, three of whom survived to adulthood. Catherine, born in the spring of 1819, was the eldest. Thomas, Alice's grandfather, arrived in July of 1821. Finally, in 1823, Mary gave birth to the Geherty's second son, Patrick.

The interior of the Geherty home was grimy with the smoke of a generation's peat fires, but the greasy residue that clung to the overhead thatch kept it more or less leak resistant and free of insects. The dirt floor, compressed by tens of thousands of footsteps, was smooth and hard. As the family slept snugly in beds of straw, the faint rustling of rodents emanated from dark corners. The cottage's stone walls were rough and cold on the inside, and irregularly spattered on the outside with delicate green mosses and lichens, an indication of Westmeath's damp environment.

Rarely was Thomas, the elder of the weaver's scrawny sons, warm when he awoke or satisfied when his plate had been scraped clean. In fact, Thomas Geherty was hungry much of his life. Even so, tenant farmers in the area would have been envious of the weaver's relative prosperity. Linen weaving, an ancient craft requiring considerable knowledge and skill, usually ensured a slightly higher standard of living than tending the crops of Ireland's English landlords.

Ireland's peasant farmers worked the fields belonging to their English masters until they were spent. Then they trudged home to tend their own meagre allotments. Legislation, originating in England, prohibited the once traditional transfer of land to the eldest son when his da passed away. As generations slipped one after the other into history, sons divided their father's legacy equally, and allocated plots of land grew smaller. By the 1840's, most were barely large enough to support even a modestly sized household. On such tiny allotments, few crops could provide sustenance for a family, and while English landowners grew wheat and raised beef for export, their Irish tenants were forced to grow potatoes to survive. They ate potato bread for breakfast, potato soup at their mid-day meal, and boiled potatoes for supper – *and gave thanks to Jesus Christ.*

The Irish famine of 1845 through 1847 was Western Europe's greatest nineteenth century human disaster. Its impact on Ireland's peasants was a direct result of their nearly exclusive dependence on potatoes.

Europe's first potato arrived from South America in the late sixteenth century. Though more nutritious than European bread and cereal diets of the period, the consumption of potatoes didn't immediately enjoy popularity. For a century, the tubers remained animal fodder and food for none but the poorest of peasants. The Irish were among the first to adopt the import as their primary food in response to the plant's high yield and its compatibility with their cool, wet climate. Even so, 65,000 Irish died as a result of the food shortage that followed *the year without a summer*. Much worse was to come.

CHAPTER TWO

THOMAS'S BURDEN

By the time of Thomas Geherty's birth, the superior varieties of potatoes had long been degraded through cross pollination. The resulting *lumper* was a wretched thing, course and susceptible to blight. Still, it was essential to Irish peasants who possessed insufficient land to grow crops of lesser yields, and equally so to Westmeath's linen weavers who could afford little else.

As a six-year-old child, Thomas stood barefoot in the village square and witnessed the completion of St. Michael's Church of Ireland, the construction of which had begun a year before his birth. The enormous cost of building the great church was funded primarily by the Pollard family. It stands today, a symbol of the disparity between aristocrats and commoners in the early nineteenth century. Memorials, some of which date from the 1750s, occupy the church's interior. They were relocated from the nearby, and now derelict and roofless, Killafree Church, but the weaver's Roman Catholic son never saw them because St. Michael's is an Anglican Church. Nevertheless, Thomas marvelled at the size and grandeur of the new building, unsurpassed in his experience until he made his arduous journey to Ireland's coastal capital almost two decades later.

Potato blight appeared in eastern North America in 1843 and spread throughout the continent over the next two years. In 1845, Ireland's predominantly cloudy, cold and wet summer foreshadowed the blight's arrival. Somehow, the destructive spores reached Europe in mid-summer, and by early September, the first signs of the disease appeared near Dublin. Through an arbitrary patchwork of darkening foliage, more than a third of Ireland's potatoes were subsequently contaminated before they could be harvested.

Jewels of dew sparkled in the early morning sunlight, as the first Westmeath peasants to be affected by the scourge emerged from their cottages. The lush potato plants, a rich green the previous day, had begun withering and turning black during the night. Each morning thereafter, farmers arose to find the blight had crept farther across their little fields. Fearful anticipation swept through County Kildare, Meath and Westmeath. Peter's neighbours dug into the damp soil beneath the dead and dying plants. In many cases, the slimy black pulp they found was utterly inedible. Desperate with panic, most families exhumed their entire crops prematurely, but large numbers of the tubers were already fetid, vile, and "frightening to look upon." Within a fortnight, the hopes of some families were completely lost. For them, there would be nothing to eat until the following summer – and perhaps not even then. Millions prayed, begging for divine intervention in the face of almost certain death. *God ignored their pleas.*

Though Peter's family relied on flax and the linen market to provide their meagre income, their diet differed little from that of their neighbours, and economically, they too were dependent on the humble potato for their sustenance. Aside from special occasions, Peter's children had seldom tasted cheese or meat. Another economic factor, the industrial revolution, contributed to the plight of the Geherty family. Steam power and technological advances in weaving machinery were encouraging the centralization of Ireland's weaving industry in Belfast. Industrialization was proving more efficient, and incomes in the cottage industry of spinners and weavers were declining. By the 1840s, as aging weavers' eyes dimmed, their sons were less inclined to assume their das' trade.

Families hurriedly scraped together what they could to send their eldest sons to America in pursuit of work. Some sold their only pig or cow to pay the fare – others; their few bits of wooden furniture. Many emigrant sons died of typhus in cramped steerage aboard the very ship that had promised salvation. Others survived the passage but contracted the disease and died shortly after landing in America while their families waited in vain for news of them.

Those families who couldn't afford the £3 fare, trusted their sons' fates to England's industrial economy. Passage aboard a steam packet from Dublin to Holyhead in Wales took just hours and cost only a shilling or so. In fact, some colliers unloaded their coal in Irish ports and took on human cargo as ballast for the return journey to England or Wales. Though free, passage in the hold of a collier among hundreds of tightly packed bodies exposed emigrants to body lice, potential carriers of typhus. Many came down with fever within days of the crossing, but not before seeding the rooming houses of Holyhead and Liverpool with the parasites that had infected them. The responsibility of rescuing their parents and siblings from potential starvation weighed heavily on these young men as they surrendered the security of their Irish homes. Thomas Geherty, Alice's grandfather, was among them.

> Thomas Geherty's migration to England may not have been intended as a permanent relocation. He may have planned to work there only until his family had recovered from the famine, or return to Castlepollard with enough money to buy land. Perhaps he had no plan at all, but was simply reacting to an economic crisis. In any case and for whatever reason, by remaining in England's capital until his death, he ensured that his granddaughter, Alice, was born a Londoner.

In the early nineteenth century, such a journey was, at the very least, unusual. Most ordinary people died in the same community in which they had been born, sometimes without ever seeing the pavements of a city. At twenty-four years of age, Peter and Mary's eldest son, carrying only a handful of personal possessions and a modicum of hope, joined thousands of impoverished emigrants fleeing Ireland.

On the eve of his departure, Thomas lay awake much of the night. The impenetrable black of the cottage interior amplified his ma's faint sobbing. Though he agonized over leaving her and everything familiar to him, he understood the inevitability of his journey.

The sun had barely risen when Peter grasped his son's hand and shook it firmly. Though both men knew the gesture was likely to be the last they shared, no words were spoken. Instead, they simply looked into each other's eyes for a second or two. Thomas kissed his mother's tear-stained cheek tenderly. As reluctant as he was to leave, he turned away and trod the dusty road southward toward Mullingar amid the long shadows of early morning. Just once, the young Geherty looked over his shoulder through tears that robbed him of a last, clear image of his ma.

Moments later Thomas strode past fields where the familiar blue, five-petal flax blossoms had recently flourished. Never again would he see the things he had taken for granted since infancy. With each footfall, the young man increased the distance between himself and his memories. He had been to

Mullingar twice before; once with his da to buy a cow when he was five or six, and again at his ma's insistence to seek a doctor when he broke his left leg in 1832. On that occasion, he had bounced along the rutted boreen in a borrowed handcart pulled by Patrick, his younger brother. He winced and cried out with every jerk and jolt. Like distant lightning, the memory of that day flashed into his consciousness as he retraced the route.

Into the early nineteenth century, travel between Ireland's communities relied on locally funded parish roads. Every parishioner was bound to contribute a few days labour per year to help maintain them. The byways, often impassable during inclement weather, were little more than winding dirt paths, suited to foot traffic, two-wheeled carts, and one-horse carriages. Peter had advised his son to avoid the Dublin Road through nearby Collinstown where he had been baptized in 1823. Instead, he had been encouraged to walk to Mullingar and follow the Royal Canal to the coast to avoid the tolls and reduce his chance of being set upon and robbed.

Thomas limped from the path in response to the sound of overtaking hooves. A black coupé, pulled by a lone chestnut, rattled by in a cloud of dust. The unseen occupant might have been an English merchant, a local landowner, his lady, or perhaps an official of the Church of Ireland. Whoever they were, they took no notice of the anonymous peasant walking the narrow parish road, nor the powdery dust produced by the carriage's passing. Absorbed by beads of perspiration on Thomas's face and forearms, it soon dried into a translucent layer of umber-coloured road grime. The whirring, spoked wheels clattered across a planked bridge and disappeared beyond a bend in the road. The morning silence, measured only by the young man's footfalls, resumed.

Thomas's eyes scanned the Irish countryside as he walked, but he paid it little attention as his mind was occupied by memories of his childhood. His legs maintained their repetitive motion without conscious thought, and his ears and nostrils gathered bird songs and the scents of peat smoke and wild flowers. By mid-day, his purposeful pace had carried him over Mullingar's Scanlon Bridge. At Main Street, he turned eastward as his da had instructed and walked toward Moran Bridge. Shop fronts and alleys held no attraction for young Geherty. Progress was all that mattered to him at this early stage of his journey. At the bridge, he descended the steep embankment to join the towpath of the Royal Canal which would lead him to Dublin, still more than fifty miles distant.

Thomas was somewhat fatigued by his own ambitious strides, and in spite of the extra potato bread his ma had encouraged him to eat at breakfast, he felt a little peckish. Though tempted by a second portion of bread, wrapped in a freshly laundered handkerchief and tucked into the linen bag he carried, he resolved to save it for his supper.

"I'll have it when the day's journey has ended," he whispered to himself.

A second later, it occurred to him that everything he owned was in that bag, and yet he had carried it effortlessly throughout the morning.

Canal boats, thickly painted in rich reds, greens and black, slid silently along the canal. Only the occasional rattle of a boat-horse's harness competed with the trill of blue tits and chaffinches.

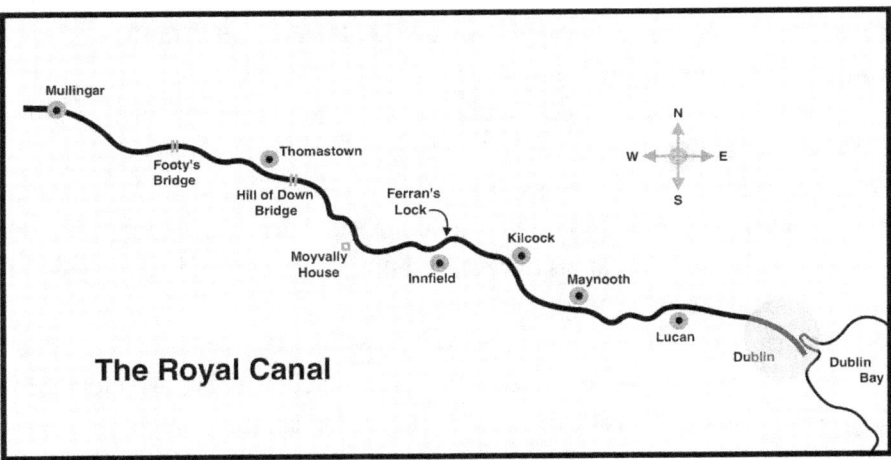

Thomas enjoyed the walk over the next seven miles, casually acknowledging the narrowboat crews as they passed. Though the canal sparkled brightly in the afternoon sun, much of the towpath was shaded by overhanging branches of ash and oak trees. By mid-afternoon, with his legs growing weary and his resolve waning, he slumped onto a grass embankment beneath Footy's Bridge and closed his eyes. He couldn't help himself. He had walked more than eighteen miles in eight hours with hardly a pause along the way, and every joint below his waist ached. He luxuriated in their stillness while the beating of his heart slowed. Dream-like images of those he'd left behind ebbed and flowed through his thoughts. They would soon face the hardships of winter with fewer resources than ever before, unprecedented potato prices, and little to eat.

His idleness felt inappropriate, even irresponsible, and he knew he would have to continue.

"In a minute," he breathed.

Eventually, Thomas found the will to struggle to his feet and resume his quest. Over the next hour and a half, he passed a series of eight locks on his gradual descent toward Dublin. His pace slowed, he began favouring his left leg a little more than usual, and he stopped frequently to catch his breath. East of Thomastown, just beyond lock eighteen in County Kildare, the young adventurer turned and watched the autumn sun sink toward Westmeath. Songbirds slipped into silence, and traces of evening fog began settling over the canal. Thomas sat down with his back against the trunk of an ancient wych elm, consumed the last of his ma's bread, and gathered his coat tightly around his body. There, isolated from everything dear and familiar, he slept rough throughout the moonless night.

The morning dawned cool and overcast. Young Geherty awoke chilled through and stiff, relieved himself behind a nearby bush, and returned to the towpath. With only a few coins to sustain him through a fortnight of travel, he had been determined to walk as much of the journey as possible, but the first day had eaten away at his resolve, and the bitter night air had robbed him of sleep. He was as tired as he had ever been.

Thomas tried dutifully to maintain the previous day's pace as he plodded along a level stretch of canal lined with brilliant yellow gorse. At mid-morning, while passing beneath the Hill of Down Bridge, the thought of buying passage on a canal boat tugged at his willpower. He brushed the idea aside and continued eastward. Much of the surrounding terrain was hidden by the greenery that lined the canal though even the smallest communities were betrayed by aging stone bridges linking the north and south banks. Noon was approaching by the time he reached Moyvally House, nine miles from the place where he had slept. A few cottages lined the road a short distance south of the canal. Thomas walked toward them purposefully. Within a few minutes, he acquired valuable intelligence about the area. A local advised that he was still thirty miles or so from Dublin's docks, but more importantly, she confided that bread might be obtained from a baker at Innfield, a mere three or four miles to the east.

A little more than an hour later, Thomas retrieved a George III half-penny from his purse to purchase a small loaf of bread. Yet another horse-drawn narrowboat passed as he approached the towpath on blistered and burning feet. With two thirds of the loaf stuffed into his bag for later, he gnawed on the smaller portion.

Lined with stone that had been chiselled and fitted with precision, Ferran's Lock went almost unnoticed as the young man's eyes focused on the next bend in the canal – *always on the next bend*. It wasn't yet supper-time when he found himself at the sixteenth lock at Kilcock, but he could go no further. He wandered into the market town in the hope of discovering a place to sleep. Not far from the canal, he came upon a Roman Catholic Chapel and removed his cap.

Thomas Geherty entered respectfully, knelt and crossed himself before sitting in the rear pew as far from the door as possible. He offered a prayer of thanks for his progress and appealed to his saviour for strength. He closed his eyes for just a moment and thought about his ma, the bed he had shared with his siblings, and the smell of his da's smouldering pipe. He recalled the soothing warmth of the family's peat fire in the evening. His memories overlapped and intertwined, then merged with peat smoke and dissolved into nothingness.

Thomas awoke with a start in absolute darkness.

"Where am I?" he thought.

Seconds slipped by as he struggled to comprehend, and then it came to him. He had fallen asleep in a chapel in Kilcock. He sat up, wondered what the hour was, and cautiously looked around in the darkness. Faint pinpoints of light shone through a small window high above his left shoulder. His hip felt bruised where it had been pressed against the bench. He shifted his position slightly and closed his eyes.

Thomas's third day began with an overwhelming sense of hopelessness. It overtook him like the shadow of a cloud on a moonlit winter night. The rhythmic clatter of his da's loom echoed in the recesses of his memory. He had grown up listening to that sound. It was as familiar to him as his own heartbeat, and now it was gone; perhaps never to be heard again. He wanted desperately to retrace his steps to the sweet comfort of his family's cottage. His ma's warm embrace, now a mere recollection, blurred his vision for a second time.

Kilcock's grey streets glistened under a light morning drizzle. A handful of villagers moved purposefully this way and that, attending to unnamed tasks of undetermined significance. Dejected, Thomas returned to the towpath on the Royal Canal's north bank, turned his back on Dublin and walked a hundred yards west to Shaw Bridge. From the bridge, overlooking Lock Sixteen, he spied a distant narrowboat approaching from the west. A boy and a sturdy white boat-horse plodded steadily toward him. The latter, tugging intermittently on a rope attached to the boat's masthead looby, appeared indifferent to the rain. Icy droplets trickled down Thomas's neck onto his back as he studied the approaching vessel. He descended the bank and sheltered beneath the arched stone structure out of the wet. There, the canal was more than fourteen feet lower than it was west of the lock. He chewed on a chunk of squished bread and thought about the twenty or so miles separating Kilcock and the ferry docks in Dublin. He dreaded the torturous walk and prayed for strength, but Thomas felt only weakness and despair.

Narrowboat navigating the Royal Canal.

The creak of the lock gate signalled that the narrowboat was about to enter the stone-lined basin above Thomas's head. He climbed the bank and watched as the sixty-foot boat eased into the lock. The boatman, dressed in a striped shirt, a waistcoat and a red neckerchief, tipped his dripping hat. He looked approachable. Unable to resist the opportunity another minute, Thomas succumbed to the temptation and began negotiating passage to Dublin.

"I beg your pardon, sir," he began, "Are you going to Dublin City, then?"

"Aye," responded the boatman.

Thomas paused; then, awkwardly blurted out the purpose of his inquiry.

"Might you take me there? I'll be paying, to be sure."

Initially, the boatman hesitated, but the opportunity to add to his day's wages was more than he could resist.

"Sixpence then."

Thomas counted out the fare and watched as the boatman put the coins into his purse.

"Step aboard, lad."

The boatman introduced himself as Patrick Lynch, and invited his passenger to sit on a bench inside the cabin. Mr Lynch stood just aft of the hatches with one hand on the tiller.

"Is that your son?" Thomas queried, nodding in the direction of the narrowboat's bow.

"That he is. Thirteen years and been leading Ahearn for almost a year now," replied Mr Lynch.

"Ahearn?" Thomas probed.

The boatman's countenance filled with pride. "Ahearn, yes. It means lord of the horses."

Thankful to be out of the rain, the young Geherty watched the sodden landscape slide past a circular portlight. The rain persisted, but the day passed easily for him, dry and distracted as he was by his conversation with the boatman. He learned that the unseen cargo beneath the peaked wooden deck was grain, bound for the docks in Dublin, and he discovered the boy's mother had "gone to Heaven" when he was born. He'd begun working with his father out of necessity after his grandmother died the previous autumn. Thomas, occupied by thoughts of his *own* mother, grew quiet.

CHAPTER THREE

STEAM PACKETS AND STAGE COACHES

By late afternoon, the rain had passed though thick, low cloud-cover persisted. Thomas stood alongside Mr Lynch, watching Dublin approach through the gloom. The stench of the city and the fishy scent of the sea enveloped the boat as a single odour. As both smells were foreign to him, he found the combination rather unpleasant.

Brick and stone took the place of the yellow gorse and green foliage Thomas had admired along the canal's banks since Mullingar. Rows of windows, stacked one atop the other, challenged the height of St. Michael's Church. Thomas felt strangely disoriented by the city's overwhelming presence.

While still a half-mile from the River Liffey, the narrowboat entered *Lock One* at the Newcomen Bridge.

"Well lad," announced the boatman, "This place is where we take our leave."

Mr Lynch had young Geherty's sixpence in his pocket, and didn't want to risk his employer seeing a passenger on the company boat. Thomas nodded and stepped ashore.

"Good day Sir! And God be with you."

Dublin, where the weak autumn sun touched it, was drying out. Thomas leaned against a high stone wall for a few minutes, watched the narrowboat clear the lock, and devoured the last of the loaf he had purchased at Innfield the previous day. Mr Lynch had suggested that he make his way to North Wall Quay on the Liffey, where the office of The City of Dublin Steam Packet Company would be found.

"Just stay on the left bank all the way, and you'll do well," the boatman advised.

Thomas glanced furtively around, withdrew his purse from his coat, and counted his remaining coins. Taking great care to avoid dropping any, he returned them to his pocket and began walking. The steamer fare to Wales would cost him dearly, but there was work waiting in London. He followed the canal to the sea lock where the Royal Canal ended at the River Liffey and turned left along the river's northern bank.

> Ireland became part of Britain through the Act of Union in 1801 and remained so until partition in 1921. As a result, migrants travelling from Ireland to England in 1845 were not documented, and since ferry operators didn't compile passenger lists, there is no written record of young Thomas Geherty's crossing of the Irish Sea.

The weaver's son was prepared to pay the ten pence steerage fare to Holyhead when he learned that thruppence would buy his passage if he didn't mind being restricted to the ferry's open deck. Impulsively, he accepted the offer and boarded the steam packet. Once on deck, he encountered a mere handful of others who shared his naive approach to the crossing. Most of the passengers had paid the full fare and had gone below where tightly packed sleeping accommodations awaited them. Thomas watched as several carriages and wagons were hoisted on deck and bound in place with heavy lashings of rope. He eyed the bindings and began to wonder about the wisdom of his decision.

As the sun dipped beyond the hills west of the city, a cool sea-breeze swept the afternoon warmth from the harbour. Thomas shivered in the fading light. He plunged his hand into the bag he'd carried more than sixty miles and felt blindly for a course linen neckcloth that his ma had made for him. He withdrew it, wrapped it about his neck, and glanced apprehensively toward the Irish Sea.

The sea's insatiable taste for human life was legendary. Shipwrecks were regularly reported and discussed over a pint throughout the British Isles; even in inland villages such as Castlepollard. The Union was, after all, an island nation, entirely dependent on shipping for transportation, trade, and defence. Everyone, it seemed, knew someone who had perished at sea. First-hand accounts of coastal wrecks were popular tales in pubs and coaching inns.

"Cast off the port bow line!" shouted an unseen officer.

The seventeen-year-old steam packet *Gypsy* sailed for Holyhead with the tide shortly after ten in the evening. She was barely beyond the mouth of the

A City of Dublin Steam Packet typical of the 1840s

River Liffey when cold winds swirled over her deck, lashing Thomas and his fellow adventurers with salt-laden spray. The deck leaned noticeably as they sought shelter in the lee of a wooden crate. The transition from sunny harbour to windswept seascape unsettled Thomas. Howling headwinds tore at his clothes as scudding clouds, backlit by the moon, exaggerated the ferry's progress. The hours passed slowly, and the merciless cold penetrated his bones. Sleep was impossible, as was conversation with anyone other than God Himself.

The deck passengers huddled uncomfortably against the base of the crate throughout the night. As the first hints of daylight crept above the eastern horizon, the wind's anger began to ease. Thomas thought he could distinguish a dark line between the sea and the sky off the steam packet's bow. He studied it thoughtfully for several minutes until it solidified in the early dawn.

"That must be Wales," he thought.

It was.

As the *Gypsy* bumped against Admiralty Pier, dockworkers seized the ferry's heavy hawsers and scurried about, looping them over squat iron bollards. Unlike Dublin with its maze of tightly packed warehouses and factories, the port of Holyhead appeared primitive and insignificant. Within a few minutes, Thomas strode down the gangplank into the community of 6,000 souls, bigger than Castlepollard but miniscule compared to the city of Dublin. He hoped to find a nearby inn, but his initial inquiries were met with blank looks and shrugs. The dockworkers, fully occupied with their duties, spoke Brythonic Welsh and had difficulty understanding his Westmeath Irish. A short walk from the wharf, he turned into Holyhead's Boston Street and came upon a coaching inn signboard. Carved gilt letters spelled, "*The Feathers*" against the black-painted board. Weary from his sleepless crossing of Muir Éireann, Thomas entered the doorway beneath the sign. Griff Krueger greeted him in English and offered a night's lodging and an evening meal for 1s. 4d. It seemed a dear price to Thomas, but he was glad to be out of the weather, if only for the night, and withdrew the required amount from his purse. His supper of boiled mutton, onions and maip was served in silence by Jane, the innkeeper's wife who apparently spoke only Welsh. Thomas chewed the meat with great enthusiasm. He had consumed the last of his bread the previous day, and was less than satisfied when his plate was empty. As he sipped on a hot cup of tea, Mrs Krueger turned to her husband and spoke a few words in Welsh.

The man responded, "*Iawn*."

With a hint of a motherly smile, the innkeeper's wife put a thick slice of dense bread on Thomas's plate.

"God bless you," Thomas murmured.

Though it was common for travellers of the time to find themselves sharing a bed with a stranger, Thomas enjoyed a good night's sleep with a bed all to himself. He awakened the following morning refreshed and eager to be on the road again. Griff Krueger served him a bowl of steaming oatmeal for sixpence, gave him directions to the London Road on the other side of the harbour, and sent him on his way with a nod.

The London Road was unlike anything Thomas had ever experienced. It had been completed in 1826 in response to the Act of Union. With London at one end and Holyhead at the other, it provided a direct connection between England's capital and Dublin. In contrast to the deeply rutted, muddy laneways of Castlepollard Parish, its fine stone surface was level, smooth and firm. It suited carriage wheels perfectly, but the unyielding surface was hard on the feet of pedestrians. Thomas resumed his journey with purpose and determination.

Eight hours into his pursuit of London, Thomas reached the Pont Grog y Borth, a chain suspension bridge spanning the Menai Strait. It had been constructed while he was still a toddler, but he had neither seen nor imagined anything like it before. He stood staring in awe for several minutes, unable to fully comprehend what he was seeing. Gingerly, he looked down into the chasm between Anglesey and the mainland. Glistening swells rolled beneath a handful of vessels a hundred feet below the roadway. A web of chains and black iron stretched through space to the hills beyond the strait. Massive limestone towers stood at each end of a 560-foot span of roadway. The thought of crossing the bridge was terrifying.

A mail coach raced noisily past Thomas on its dash toward London. Within a few seconds, it had crossed the gap and disappeared from view. Thomas heard only the wind and the squeal of waterfowl far below. He felt very alone and wished his da could have been there to answer the questions he had about the bridge. Tentatively, he walked forward a few steps and stopped. His legs felt weak. He crossed himself and continued slowly out onto the bridge, passing warily beyond the first tower. He fixed his eyes on the planked road ahead and increased his pace until, by the time he had passed beneath the second tower, he was almost running.

Thomas tingled with adrenalin as he continued on his way to Shrewsbury, ninety miles east of Holyhead. He wondered if there would be more bridges like Pont Grog y Borth on the road to London. Shadows grew longer as the day progressed, and he began thinking about a suitable place to sleep.

Perhaps I'll come upon a derelict cottage or a cowshed, he thought.

> Thomas Geherty's journey to the great city of London left no footprints among the records of the nineteenth century. Nor were accounts of his emigration passed down through the family. The details of his discomfort, loneliness and anxieties are destined to remain lost among the shadows of past generations forever.

Far from his home for the first time in his life, Thomas's enthusiasm for adventure began to wane. When he thought about his family, as he frequently did, he felt isolated and anxious though he couldn't specifically identify what it was that he feared. Day after day, Thomas trudged through Wales and into England. The walking was easy on the modern roadway though his feet and legs always ached by mid-day. At Shrewsbury, after a week of sleeping along the road, a coaching inn called *The Lion* provided sustenance and a warm bed for the night.

Shrewsbury was an important town on the road to England's capital. It's population in the fall of 1845 was about 19,000, and its inhabitants welcomed the dozen or so travellers who passed through it each day. Thomas found the *The Lion* a little intimidating. He was fully aware of his dishevelled and dirty appearance, but the innkeeper didn't seem to take notice. With a thin potato stew and a bit of bread in his belly, Thomas retired for the night in a tiny room at the top of a narrow stairway. With barely enough room to stand up or turn around, he removed his outer clothing and rested his weary bones on a mattress stuffed with feathers. It was a new and luxurious experience that wasn't often repeated during his lifetime.

On awakening, Thomas tallied his coins three times, hoping in vain that he had somehow miscounted. It would take almost every well-worn pence in his purse to reach London by coach, but walking would surely take him another week, and by then, he would have spent everything he had on food. Besides, he reasoned, the quicker he reached his destination, the sooner he could begin work and start earning a wage. Once again, he succumbed to fatigue and impatience, resolving to ride to London in a coach if the fare didn't exceed his current worth.

Thomas arranged his transport, paid the fare and slumped onto a rough-hewn bench in the inn courtyard to await the coach's arrival. Though the sun shone through the clouds periodically, the day's character was mainly overcast and blustery.

As fresh horses were put to the whippletree by the liveryman, Thomas stepped up and into a carriage for the first time in his life.

"Good day ta ya!" greeted a fellow Irishman who, by all appearances, shared a similar social standing.

"Good day, sir," said Thomas.

"Are ya goin' ta London, then?"

"I am," replied Thomas.

"My name's Deoradhán, John Deoradhán," declared the stranger as he thrust a gnarly hand toward Thomas.

Thomas grasped the man's hand and pumped it, warily engaging his flickering eyes in the half-light of the coach's interior.

"Thomas Geherty of Castlepollard," he stated formally as he took the seat opposite the man.

The coach lurched when the horses responded to the driver's "g'yup!"

For a time, Thomas was occupied with the newness of the experience. Leaves brushed against the vehicle as it jostled and bumped past the yellowing buckthorns that grew along the road to Birmingham. Wood squeaked against wood somewhere behind Thomas's head, and harness fittings rattled. John Deoradhán, obviously as new to coach travel as young Geherty, commented on the speed at which the stage coach was moving. Soon, the two men were chatting casually above the din, recounting their respective journeys to Shrewsbury and sharing their hopes for the days to come. After an hour or so, they became comfortable with one another's company and spoke less frequently. Then, they closed their eyes and dozed as the coach swayed and bounced toward its destination.

Thomas's eyes snapped open when the horses stopped abruptly in the muddy yard of Birmingham's *Hen and Chickens Inn*. He looked about to see where he was; then followed his fellow traveller out of the coach and into the inn. The two men had travelled forty miles together in a little more than five hours, a distance that would have taken Thomas two days to walk. Still, he wondered if his da would have approved of him spending most of his money on transportation when he had two serviceable legs with which to walk.

Thomas and John sat down on a well-worn bench, and gulped local ale while they awaited their evening meal. When their supper was placed in front of them, it was neither hot nor very tasty. In fact, Thomas speculated whether it might be better left on the plate, but he was too hungry to entertain the idea long. The innkeeper appeared indifferent to their presence, speaking only when addressed directly. Thomas began to wonder if his Irish accent might be the cause of the man's behaviour. The idea would grow to become a firm conviction over the next couple of years.

Both men ate quickly before being shown to a tiny windowless room where they were to sleep for a few hours. The bed was not very comfortable, but it was far better than sleeping in a cow shed, and much sweeter smelling.

The pair awoke to loud banging that caused the room's door to rattle in its frame. It was time to continue their journey. In the half-light of early morning, they were instructed to sit on an outside seat as the coach's interior was already occupied. One after the other, they climbed up to take their places for the next segment of the journey. A third man, an Englishman who claimed the far end of the bench behind the driver, looked up from his Birmingham Gazette and nodded coldly.

The driver and his passengers jerked and jiggled throughout the uncomfortable fourteen-hour rush toward London. Only brief stops allowed for refreshment while the horses were being changed at inns along the way. The sun had set long before the coach wound its way through the boroughs north of London. Sore and exhausted on arrival at the *Swan with Two Necks Inn* on Lad Lane in Cheapside, Thomas and John wished each other well and abruptly dispersed into the darkened streets of London.

Thomas, suddenly alone and almost penniless, found himself bewildered and looking for some indication of where to go. Just a short walk from Wren's St. Paul's Cathedral, surrounded by brick and stone, he stood frozen by his own indecision. Aside from the shadows cast by rows of gaslights, the streets were almost empty, though occasionally a carriage skittered through a distant intersection.

Shivering in the damp night air, the man who would become Alice's grandfather entered an alley between Wood Street and Milk Street. There, among the shadows, he propped himself up against a cold stone wall and went to sleep.

The Swan with Two Necks Coaching Inn, Lad Lane, Cheapside

Postal service had been introduced in Ireland a mere five years earlier, but communicating through written correspondence was still uncommon among low-income people, due primarily to a high rate of illiteracy. No one in the Geherty family could properly read or write. Thomas, eight-years-old when Ireland's national education system was introduced in 1831, could read no more than a few simple words and could not even sign his own name. There was, however, a custom at that time of requesting one's priest to both read and write letters in return for a modest donation to the church. Of course, correspondence written by educated members of the

Roman Catholic priesthood did not reflect the character of the sender. On the contrary; it tended to be comparatively formal and pretentious.

Thomas carried such a letter, somewhat soiled, folded to a quarter of its size, and bearing the precious penned address of his younger brother Patrick. That piece of paper was critical to his quest. It was his sole means of finding his brother amid the two million inhabitants of London and its environs, and it was the first thing he thought about when he awoke stiff and cold the following morning.

> *September 26th 1845*
> *My Dear Father,*
> *I trust you and Mother are found well although the hunger is upon you. You must find hope in Christ Our Lord and also in Thomas's pursuit of employment in London.*
>
> *I am happy to communicate to you of a position here in the gas works, being an offer of employment suited to my dear brother's needs on the most reasonable terms. I hold not the least doubt, but it will cause a happy situation for him and benefit you exceedingly.*
>
> *I am advised that a strong and honourable man will nigh be sought to stoke fires at the manufactory. I therefore invite my dear Thomas to present himself at my home at number 2 Gas Court, Clerkenwell at his earliest opportunity, such that he might apply to Mr Samuel Clegg directly and on his own behalf.*
>
> *My compliments to my Dearest Mother and my sister Catherine and to my cousins also.*
>
> > *Your loyal son,*
> > *Patrick Geherty,*

Patrick had forsaken Castlepollard when he was seventeen and had run off to England with Mary Magane whose family lived in the nearby village of Multyfarnham. She was, at the time, pregnant with his child. With no family in London to contradict them, the young couple lied about their ages and married on 12 July 1840. Aligned with the bride's name, in the field labelled, "Rank or Profession of Father," the registrar recorded, "Dead." In the spaces provided for the signatures of the newlyweds, Patrick and Mary penned crudely drawn X's.

Patrick, one of 100,000 Irish immigrants in London at the time, found work as a gas-lamp lighter. Each evening, he meandered through the streets of Clerkenwell igniting flames which he was destined to extinguish just a few hours later. By the time Thomas arrived in London in 1845, Patrick was working as a stoker at the Cooperage Gas Works at Pear Tree Street and Brick Lane.

Somewhat road-weary and significantly scruffier than most of those he encountered, Thomas began his morning by approaching strangers in an effort to locate Patrick's residence. His Irish accent betrayed him each time, and while he didn't entirely understand the sentiment behind the strangers' rebuffs, he quickly realised that most had little interest in aiding his search. Even those who might have been sympathetic were unlikely to have known the tiny alley described in the tattered letter.

To Thomas, it was the Londoners who spoke with an accent, so when a passer-by directed a random comment to his female companion with no noticeable accent, Thomas's head jerked in their direction.

"I beg your pardon, sir! Would you be so kind as to help me, please?"

The dark-haired man wheeled around, expressionless as he awaited Thomas's request. Digging into his trouser pocket to retrieve his letter, Thomas appealed to the couple to help him find his brother's house. The man looked at the document for a long time without comment. Finally, he read the penultimate paragraph and spoke the address aloud, as if the words formed a question.

"2 Gas Court, Clerkenwell? I don't know of it, but I'll chance it's somewhere by the old gas works on Brick Lane."

"Brick Lane?" queried Thomas.

The man nodded.

"*That's* in Clerkenwell," he added.

While the woman smiled pleasantly at the immigrant, the man pointed north, suggesting that Thomas walk, "no more than two miles," in the direction indicated.

As Thomas went on his way, the woman's voice rang out from behind him.

"Look for the black, iron holders, sir."

Thomas looked over his shoulder and smiled in acknowledgement, though he had no idea what she meant by *holders*.

CHAPTER FOUR

THE IMMIGRANT

Thomas's brief exposure to Dublin's urban environment hadn't prepared him for London. He was overwhelmed by the city's cold and brutal countenance. Its endless rows of terraced flats obscured the landscape, and its cobbled pavements sealed the earth beneath his feet. A dense, claustrophobic fog swirled among passing carriages, filling his lungs with damp. In the murky morning light, rows of wrought iron gaslights patiently awaited yet another nightfall. Hawkers and costermongers hovered like predators, impatient to sell their wares to workers hurrying to nearby offices and factories. Thomas looked straight ahead and walked quickly northward. When Wood Street turned west and forked, the young Geherty stood pondering his choices. Then, for no particular reason, he took the right fork into Whitecross Street.

Thomas trudged on wearily, squinting into the distance at a shapeless splash of colour. As he neared, it solidified into a shop sign-board hovering above the heads of passers-by. On its painted surface, the words 'Rum Puncheon' revealed the premises to be a pub. The publican was sweeping debris through the doorway onto the pavement as he approached. A blend of odours, primarily tobacco-smoke and stale ale, greeted the young Irishman at the open door. The man with the broom turned and looked into Thomas's eyes expectantly.

"Might you be acquainted with Brick Lane, good sir?"

The publican lowered his head slowly as his eyes measured Thomas's status in the world. Then, without a word, he jerked his head in the direction Thomas had been walking.

"My thanks sir!"

Within minutes, Whitechurch Street came to an end at St. Luke Church, Old Street, and slightly to the west, not far away, Thomas spied a belching smoke stack and an odd-looking cylindrical ironwork structure – a *holder* he concluded.

In no time at all, the young immigrant began exploring the streets and lanes of Clerkenwell in the vicinity of the gas works. Spilling out of Great

Mitchell Street onto Brick Lane, he stood staring at the street sign for a few seconds until a passing youth confirmed the street's name. Thomas turned north confidently, and almost immediately noted an opening between the buildings on the west side. The red brick walls on either side of the narrow, dead end alley featured doors that could well have been entrances to flats.

Typical 19th century telescopic gas holders, also known as gasometers.

Might this be Gas Court? he thought.

The far end of the alley terminated at a high wooden fence of vertical planks, split and weathered by the passage of time. Thomas peered into the gas works yard through a half-inch gap. Everything beyond the fence appeared to be shades of the same colour – *industrial revolution*! Just days ago, he had lived unconstrained in the midst of open fields and green leaves and grasses, but here he felt confined by grey stone, millions of red-brown bricks, and filth. His nostrils filled with the acrid stench of industry. Thomas turned away from the fence and found himself staring into the gaze of a uniformed peeler.

"What are you up to then?" boomed the man in a black tunic and top-hat.

"I . . . I was . . . I am in search of Gas Court," he stammered as the man glared at him suspiciously.

"Why?" demanded the official.

Thomas hastened to retrieve the letter from his coat and presented it in response.

Moments later, Patrick Geherty flung open his door to find his scruffy elder brother, bag in hand, standing before him. As the two exchanged greetings and shared a hearty handshake, the unmoved constable turned away to continue his patrol of St. Luke's Parish.

Patrick Geherty's home was tiny, dark and austere, yet from Thomas's perspective it was a warm haven from the cold and indifference which he had experienced since leaving his father's cottage. Finally, he could have a real conversation about familiar things – home and family. Patrick added a little coal to the fire, and the two men sat by the hearth to talk.

Fatigued as he was from his arduous journey, Thomas lay awake much of his first night in Clerkenwell. The city's incessant murmur was a dramatic contrast to Castlepollard's moonlit silence, and the young Geherty wondered if he would ever be able to sleep again.

By seven a.m. Thomas and his brother were standing before the gas works' general manager because Mr Clegg was occupied with other business. The manager was a burley Scotsman named Duncan MacPherson who understood the desperation that motivated Irish immigrants.

"So, yer oirish, then are ye?" confirmed MacPherson.

"Yes sir," Thomas nodded.

The man studied Thomas's demeanour and made him a frugal offer. It was settled then; he would begin the following evening as a *wheeler*. He was to work twelve hours a night; six nights a week. It would be his seemingly endless task to deliver countless barrows of coal to the stokers who fuelled the insatiable furnaces. The work would be hot, backbreaking and relentless.

When Thomas arrived for his first shift, Mr MacPherson introduced him to a gas-fitter named Tom Sookin. "Tom wi' show ye 'round an' git ye ae barrow an' sheullie," he said.

The Brick Lane Gas Manufactory retort house where coal was heated in ovens to promote the release of coal gas.

The gas-fitter was barely six years older than Geherty, yet he looked near as old as Thomas's da. He was lean and hard as if sculpted from coal, and he moved like a machine, every motion practiced 10,000 times before. Coal dust accentuated the furrows of his face and neck, and droplets of sweat clung to his brow. Tom had been transported to Australia in 1834; sentenced to seven years for the theft of a gentleman's handkerchief.

"I was there," Tom said plainly, "walking with me friends, and we found it lying on the footway. I was nineteen. They took me feckin' life away. It wasn't right."

Tom knew how it felt to be alone in a strange country, far from the comforts of family and friends. He understood what Thomas was feeling during those first days in London, and the men quickly became friends.

The handful of coins Thomas's da had entrusted to him were gone by the time he wheeled his first barrow of coal. He hoped he'd be able to repay them quickly and send a shilling home occasionally to save his family from starvation.

Night after night, Thomas wheeled coal to the furnaces, where frantic tongues of flame struck at the stokers like venomous snakes. It brought to mind Father Kiernan's accounts of Satan's underworld seething with eternal fire and brimstone. Relentless heat penetrated the thinly worn soles of his boots throughout his shift. At dawn, aching with fatigue, he staggered through the gas works' gate, filthy with coal dust, oily soot, and sweat. Nonetheless, as the weeks passed, his new life became incrementally routine and *normal*.

In 1845, the vast majority of early nineteenth-century homes were lit with tallow candles or oil lamps, but neither provided adequate light by any standard, and tallow emitted unpleasant odours in addition to excessive smoke. Even though manufactured gas became available during the century's second decade, the public feared the explosive fuel and were slow to accept it as an alternative for home lighting. Still, widespread use of gas for street lighting demanded a generous and constant supply throughout the year, especially during the winter when the nights were long. Tons of coal were heated in retorts to produce the invisible gas that was collected, stored, and distributed throughout London by several enterprising companies. Every pound of every hundredweight of coal – every ton – made its way to the furnaces in the barrows of wheelers like Thomas Geherty.

Irish immigrants flooded into London throughout the 1840s. They found work at the lowest paid, dirtiest and most dangerous jobs available, and they congregated in the poorest neighbourhoods, close to odorous industries like Samuel Clegg's Brick Lane Gas Manufactory.

In the beginning, the young Irishman hoarded his meagre earnings to pay his board and send a little home to his ma, but after a while, he allowed himself a pint from time to time. There were lots of pubs in the area, but Thomas frequented the *White Horse* on Brick Lane, because both the stoker with whom he worked and Tom Sookin the gas-fitter favoured it above the others.

Coincidentally, the stoker's name was also Tom – *Tom Darcy*. Like Thomas, Darcy had been born and raised in County Westmeath. He too had come to London with little more than a vague hope for a better life. He was much larger than young Geherty, heavier and taller, and though both men were born in the same year, Thomas revered Darcy as he would an older brother. The trio became inseparable mates, well-known at the pub as *the Toms*.

The ugly London winter was long and featureless, a seemingly endless series of shifts and dreary walks to and from the coal pile. By spring, Thomas had learned to stoke the furnaces with some degree of skill, earning himself the role of stoker or *gas fireman* as they were known in the gas works' records. As a consequence, he endured temperatures of 110 degrees Fahrenheit throughout most of his shift, but on the positive side, his modest wage increased to £1/4s/6d.

> Few details of Thomas Geherty's life are sprinkled among the millions of official documents that languish in the dusty dungeons of England's record offices. Church, state, and on occasion, even commerce provides insights into the lives of ordinary people. They do so mainly through parish records, birth and marriage registrations, and census schedules. 'Gas Court,' 'Darcy' and 'Elizabeth Sookin' are all there for those who seek to find them.

Thomas knew he was loved by his parents and siblings. He was a first-born son, a family's pride and hope, but his emigration had not been a great adventure driven by a shared dream. It was a pragmatic, utilitarian response to a problem that could not be otherwise overcome. The County Westmeath village of Castlepollard had little to offer; no hope of employment and few prospects for a man who wished to find a wife and start a family. Thomas was twenty-four years old when he saw his ma for the last time, and in addition to lacking economic resources, he yearned for something else – something he couldn't quite articulate.

Elizabeth Sookin, the daughter of a deceased cow-keeper, lived with her Irish ma and three siblings at St. James Buildings, a few streets west of the gas works. She was Tom Sookin's sister, and she made her living as a hat maker at a time when many such goods were manufactured by hand in the maker's home. She was two years older than Thomas, and when her closest friend, Ann Darcy, introduced them at Christmas in 1845, she immediately took a liking to him.

After supper, the two engaged in polite conversation.

"You work with my brother, Tom, at the gasworks, don't you?" Elizabeth asked.

"As do half of the men in St. Luke's," quipped Thomas.

Elizabeth smiled and continued to probe him for details.

"Have you come directly from Ireland then?" she queried.

"I have," he replied. "from Castlepollard, County Westmeath."

Over the next few weeks, Thomas and Elizabeth unknowingly took the first tentative steps toward a shared destiny of love, poverty and heartbreak. They met frequently at the Darcy home in the months that followed, and while winter's frigid winds brought drafts and misery to the poorest inhabitants of St. Luke's Parish, they gathered with their friends around the hearth. In time, Elizabeth discovered that, because Thomas had never attended school, he was unable to communicate with his family in Ireland. She offered to write to them on his behalf, and he, more excited than embarrassed, accepted her proposal. Though she had been born in England, Elizabeth's parents were also Irish immigrants, and Thomas felt at ease in her company. Thus, they shared their pasts, their opinions and their dreams until, at some point, the two fell in love.

Elizabeth and Thomas married on the second of May in 1846, before the congregation of St. Leonard's Church, Shoreditch. Thomas's bride watched as he scratched a crude "X" beside his name in the marriage register. The couple settled into a rented one-room flat on Old Street, a short walk from the gas

A handwritten transcript of Alice's grandparents' marriage certificate.

works. The newlyweds had very few possessions of value, but they were both employed when many of their neighbours were not. Like others in St. Luke's Parish, most of whom were Irish immigrants, they barely earned enough to pay the landlord and eat regularly. Still, when his meagre wages were laid on the palm of his hand, Thomas's thoughts returned to his starving family in Westmeath.

In the summer of 1846, Ireland's potato blight arrived in July, two months earlier than it had the previous year. The wind-borne spores found every potato crop in the country, and the devastation far exceeded that of 1845. Even the most fortunate families salvaged little more than a few meals from their fields.

In the mid-nineteenth century, the lowest socio-economic class of Londoners were the Irish Roman Catholic immigrants, the vast majority of whom were illiterate. With no skills to offer, Thomas and his countrymen worked at the least desirable jobs and lived in the poorest housing. Employers, landlords and bureaucrats alike viewed them with suspicion and contempt. The brutal prejudice which these families endured for having Irish surnames was, at the time, taken for granted.

Thomas's drudgery amid the smoke and grime of the industrial revolution continued week after week, month after month, and year after year. Though he worked long hours in terrible conditions, he seldom had an extra sixpence to send home to Ireland. Shelter from the wind and rain, a place to sleep, food, and a wooden chair in which to sit was all he could expect of life. His goal was survival, and dreams of a better life seldom, if ever, entered his thoughts. Elizabeth watched from the doorway as he walked toward the gas works in the evening. She had his tea waiting when he returned in the morning and was careful not to make noise as he slept through the day.

> Irish illiteracy had lasting effects on London immigrants and their descendants. Not only did it impact their economic and social standing during their lifetimes, but it continues to make evidence of their lives elusive because clergy, registrars and bureaucrats recorded surnames in an endless variety of spellings. Geherty became Garritty, Garratty, Gerrity and Garty – even Garret and Garby. Seoken evolved into Sookin, and Magane was heard and spelled as Magaim and Regan. Thomas's brother, Patrick, fathered four children, each one of which was registered under a different surname because he and his wife were unable to provide the spelling of their family name.

Thomas's wife was glad to have his support when, on the eleventh of August, 1847, her mother, Ellen Sookin, died suddenly. Her death, at the age of fifty-eight, was totally unexpected. She had taken to her bed with severe stomach cramps on the eighth and deteriorated rapidly. When Thomas, exhausted and black with coal dust, came home from work on the morning of the twelfth, Elizabeth's tear-streaked face looked up at him.

"Ma's gone," she cried.

London, then the largest city in the world, was unable to cope with the unending accumulation of its inhabitants' waste. Residents in poor neighbourhoods, like those surrounding the gas works, were overwhelmed by their own filth. With no modern plumbing and no sewers, urban residents relied entirely on overflowing cess pools. Landlords were not inclined to pay to have them emptied, and their tenants could simply not afford the cost. Many accumulations were located in cellars, immediately below the families they served.

Though bacteria had been known to exist since the late 1600s, doctors hadn't yet made the connection between germs and disease, so the actual cause of a death was often unknown or incorrectly identified. Ellen Sookin's death certificate states that she died from diarrhoea, the primary symptom and ultimate cause of death among victims of cholera. The usually fatal disease is spread by high concentrations of Vibrio cholera bacteria in the faeces of its infected victims. Ellen Sookin's demise was not an isolated case of the disease. London was visited repeatedly by the terrifying contagion throughout the mid-nineteenth century. Most deaths were among the residents of the city's poorest neighbourhoods. A long list of communicable diseases, including small pox, measles, scarlet fever, whooping cough and typhus claimed 1,500 lives a year in Clerkenwell alone.

Child mortality rates were especially high among London's new-borns, with thirty per cent dying prior to their fifth birthday. Thomas's brother and sister-in-law had four children by late January of 1848 when Elizabeth delivered their first child. The baby was a boy whom they named *Thomas* after his father. The 1851 census reported them living at 24 Norman's Buildings, St. Luke with their two-month-old son, yet the child doesn't appear in any subsequent census records because he died an infant.

Thomas was tending a furnace at the gas works when little Nell, his daughter, took her first breath early on the morning of March 27, 1854. She was not due for another fortnight according to her mother's reckoning, but perhaps baby Nell was simply eager to be alive. The family was living at 2 Brick Lane, well within reach of the gas work's smoke and stench. Shortly after Thomas left for work the previous evening, Elizabeth sent a neighbour's lad to fetch Ann Darcy. Ann and the local mid-wife stayed with Elizabeth throughout the night and helped deliver the baby at first light. Baby Nell's delivery was not particularly difficult for the stoker's wife, but birth was an anxious time for both baby and mother in Victorian times. When Thomas came home from work, he was surprised to find his family had increased in his absence, and he was relieved that both Elizabeth and the baby were alive.

The day after Nell was born, Britain declared war on Russia, and sent 21,000 soldiers to their deaths in the Crimean War. The world was an extremely dangerous place in the mid-nineteenth century, and not just for soldiers and babies.

In the crowded and dangerous city, life and death were often close to indistinguishable – joy and grief just a breath apart. On August 28, 1854, a worried mother named Sarah, introduced terror into London's Soho district, when she emptied the watery stools of her infant daughter into the gutter. A few feet away, a neighbour offered a cheery "good morning" as she pumped water from the local, public well. It was a common practice; an innocent act that rapidly spread cholera throughout the nearby streets and alleys. Well over 400 people crammed into every acre of the city's core, and in just two weeks more than 700 died of the dreaded disease.

The well no longer exists but the pump is there still, in Broad Street which is known today as Broadwick. The handle was removed by Dr John Snow in a desperate effort to prevent the spread of the relentless disease. The pump, now a memorial to London's ugly past, often goes unnoticed as tourists pass by on their way to and from the nearby pub – *the John Snow*.

Over a period of seven years, from 1852 to 1859, cholera killed 23,000 Britons, more than 10,000 of them within the City of London. Had Thomas and Elizabeth not been spared, Alice would never have existed.

As a working-class Victorian family, the Gehertys were never able to afford a home of their own. They were destined instead to live modestly in cramped rented flats. By Christmas of 1856 they were living at 74 Pear Tree Street, across the road from the gas works. It was their fourth matrimonial address, each of which were located within a five-minute walk of Thomas's work. It was a matter of convenience, but equally important was the fact that rents near the gas works were low. Few chose to live within reach of the manufactory's noxious fumes without a good reason. They permeated the very bricks and cobbles of the neighbourhood, and it was no secret that some gas workers, stokers in particular, suffered from diseases of the lungs within their first decade on the job. Elizabeth had already noticed that Thomas was having difficulty breathing, and occasional fits of coughing awakened him from his sleep.

Because Elizabeth gave birth to a son four days before Christmas, the Gehertys celebrated the 1856 holiday with somewhat more enthusiasm than usual. Nineteenth-century families attached great importance to the passing of a father's name on to the next generation, even when it meant re-using the name of a child who had died in infancy. Perhaps naming a second son *Thomas* was a futile grasp at immortality or simply all Thomas Geherty had to pass on to future generations.

A decade earlier, no obstacle could suppress Thomas and Elizabeth's enthusiasm for life – neither their persistent poverty, nor the pain of losing a child. They had embraced their future with hope and the naivety of youth, but through the intervening years the twinkle slowly ebbed from Elizabeth's pale blue eyes. By the fall of 1859, when the couple welcomed Alice's father into the family, she was tired, sickly and vulnerable.

CHAPTER FIVE

A CHILD OF ST. LUKE'S

In 1859, London was the largest city in the world, wealthy and prosperous, yet a desperately cruel environment from the perspective of its disadvantaged. In contrast to the simultaneous opulence of Queen Victoria's Court, the narrow lanes and alleys of St. Luke's Parish were wretched and cheerless as were the stark one-room flats of its poor. Charles Dickens's brilliant analysis, "It was the spring of hope, it was the winter of despair," was published that very year – the same year that Alice's father inhaled his first breath of London air.

In the early hours of the twentieth of September in the fifty-ninth year of the century, a bitter autumn wind rattled windows and clawed at slates and chimney pots. The baritone bell of the parish church sounded twice. The rented flat at number twelve Rose Street was as dark, as drab, and as draughty as it had ever been. A ha'penny candle flickered weakly on a table, projecting caricatures of the flat's occupants onto the room's grimy walls. Little Nell's eyes, wide with apprehension and fear, stared transfixed at a bed in the far corner where her mother gasped and whimpered in pain. Three-year-old Tom wrapped his arms around his sister and buried his face in the folds of her pinafore.

Thomas Geherty silently prayed to God to spare his wife and her baby while Elizabeth lamented that her late mother, Ellen, was not there to help with the birth. Instead, an aging midwife, a neighbour, helped her and her unborn son through their ordeal. The weakest of cries announced the arrival of the last of the Geherty's children at forty minutes past two in the morning. Long hours of painful labour left Elizabeth limp and exhausted in the night-damp room. The midwife wrapped the new-born, gently placed him into a market basket, and took her leave of the family. The infant's helpless father, overwhelmed with anxiety, stood by his wife's bedside throughout the night. From time to time, when the noise of the whirling wind subsided, Thomas leaned close to listen for Elizabeth's faint breathing.

> Peter Christopher, the last of Elizabeth Sookin Geherty's children, plays a key role in this multi-generational story. He is, after all, destined to be Alice's much loved and respected father. As such, he becomes a major influence in the development of her values, character and personality. He is the one who will reassure her that it's okay to leave her family and emigrate to Canada with the man she loves.

Elizabeth Geherty named her baby "Peter" after Thomas's da, a man *she* never knew and *he* would never meet – "*a weaver in Ireland*" Peter was told. In fact, he didn't understand what it was like to have a grandfather, or a grandmother for that matter, as all of his grandparents were either deceased by the time of his birth or far away on the other side of the Irish Sea. Still, he was the conduit through which their genes and values flowed. He was the link between Ireland and Alice.

Forty-one-year-old Elizabeth was ill through much of her pregnancy, and the difficult delivery had an adverse effect on her health. She survived the night of Peter's birth and recovered a little, but the ordeal left her frail and sickly.

By the spring of 1861, the nomadic Geherty family had moved once more; this time to number one Pear Tree Street at the corner of Goswell Road. There, the soot from the gas work's chimney settled on the roof like fine, black snow. The stench of leaking coal-gas hung in the air. The rise and fall of a nearby storage tank, mere yards from the Geherty flat, reflected the city's nightly cycle of consumption. By sunset, it neared the top of its lattice-like iron holder, ready to supply London's light. Each morning, the huge tank sank to within a few feet of street-level, thereby enforcing the daily rhythm of Thomas Geherty's life.

Elizabeth never fully regained her health, and sadly, Peter grew up with no lasting memories of his mother. Though he was four-years-old when Elizabeth passed, his mother had, in effect, traded her life for his.

"She was never *right* after our Peter was born," said Thomas on more than one occasion. It likely never occurred to him that Peter would hear those words and forever connect her absence with his birth. As he grew toward manhood, he found himself haunted by a vague sense of loss and illusive guilt.

Death was commonplace among London's working class in the 1860s. Almost a quarter of the city's children lost a parent by the age of ten. Widows and widowers usually remarried hastily since mothers were desperate for a means of support, and fathers needed someone to care for their children. Some parents simply abandoned their offspring or terminated their education and put them to work out of necessity. As a consequence, yet another generation slipped into poverty's tenacious grasp.

While his reasons are unknown, Thomas didn't remarry after Elizabeth's death. Instead, he placed his ten-year-old daughter, Nell, in the care of his wife's sister, Julia, who along with her husband, operated the Green Gate Inn at Tottenham. There, the child earned her keep by performing the duties of a domestic servant. Thomas and his sons, young Tom and Peter, moved in with the Darcy family who lived nearby on Waterloo Street. Ann Darcy, already occupied with the care of her own family, did what she could to offset Elizabeth's absence. For a decade or so, Peter looked to her for maternal guidance and developed a close bond with the Darcy family.

Peter Geherty was a Victorian child and a London boy. He faced unique challenges of geography and time; *geography* because London's manufacturing neighbourhoods were filthy, terrible places to live; and *time* because of the social and economic oppression of Irish Roman Catholics in the mid-nineteenth century. Peter's immersion in the Irish working-class enclave of St. Luke's, Old Street, offered little hope of escaping Dickens's "winter of despair." He wore his inherited name and accent like a World War II yellow star of David, marking him as unworthy of respect and opportunity.

Not only was Peter motherless, and thus deprived of the care and nurturing that only a mother can bestow, but he was in many respects fatherless as well. When Elizabeth died a few winters after Peter's birth, Thomas was unable to care for his children as *she* had. Most of his time outside of work was allocated to sleep, and what remained didn't allow for the proper nurturing of his children.

Thomas, having recently lost his wife, the one comfort that London had afforded him, withdrew into self-pity. When he wasn't stoking furnaces at the gas works or asleep in his comfortless bed, he was most often found at *The White Horse*, quaffing a pint with his co-workers and talking politics. Thomas wasn't a brutal father in the physical sense, but his absence had a brutal impact on his motherless children.

While society was moving haltingly toward modernization and social responsibility, those living in the filthy slums of St. Luke's were unlikely to have noticed. The education of mid-Victorian children was, at best, a haphazard process. Independent schools offered classes for a modest sum, but most parents in St. Luke's simply couldn't afford the fees. Some children acquired basic literacy skills by attending Sunday Schools though often the poorest children didn't own clothes decent enough to attend. *Ragged schools*, designed to accommodate those who might otherwise go uneducated, began to appear in London about 1845. They were founded, organized and staffed by unpaid volunteers and generally offered trades training to prepare children for employment. Some ragged schools provided meals and clothing to those in need. Still, many of the children of the parish's labourers were more likely to be found at work than at school.

Legislation prohibited children under fourteen from working for more than twelve hours a day, and those under nine years of age could not legally be employed in factories. Many of them, however, found work hawking merchandise on London's streets. Among other things, they sold newspapers, matches and fruit. Others worked in the dimly-lit and poorly-heated flats in which they lived, out of sight of those who were concerned about child exploitation. They made matches, or artificial flowers for the millinery industry, or cut, folded and glued boxes. Mid-century box-makers, most eight to ten years old, could earn up to four shillings a week.

Peter's earliest income came from running errands for neighbours and nearby shop owners. It was sporadic work, but errands paid thruppence on average and could add up to two or three shillings by week's end. Occasionally, he and his mates gathered coal along the tracks of the London-Manchester Southern Railway and sold their booty for whatever they could get. By the time he reached eight years of age, little Peter was working as a milk delivery helper. Later, he cleaned machinery and performed various other duties at J. J. Stockall & Sons' clock factory for four and sixpence a week. Because we tend to judge the past through the eyes of the present, it's important to recognize that Peter accepted things as they were – difficult to be sure, but perfectly normal from his perspective.

Peter Geherty was a curious boy. He loved exploring the nooks and crannies of the neighbourhood and assembled a detailed mental map of the area at an early age. He knew everyone for blocks around, and they knew him. Peter, the stoker's boy, the barefoot lad, the motherless kid; each had their own way of referring to him, but he was, in his own eyes, merely a London boy.

When they weren't working, Peter and his pals were generally free to do as they pleased, as long as they returned home in time for supper. Most often, their own hunger ensured compliance with *that* expectation. They chased carriages for the fun of it and raced one another to the source of distant smoke to see a building ablaze. They made balls out of discarded rags or sat on the bank of London's Regents Canal to watch the barges go by. The nearby puffing of a steam locomotive invariably distracted them from whatever else they were doing. Sometimes Peter and Ellen Darcy, who was a year older than him, just walked to King Square or Bunhill Field to sit on the grass and talk.

London's Irish-born population, most of whom believed that Ireland should become an independent republic, had peaked in 1851 to about 110,000. More Irish immigrants lived in Clerkenwell than any other part of the city, so the subject was a constant source of political discontent and debate in the local pubs.

The Fenian movement was growing wherever Irishmen lived, and St. Luke's, Clerkenwell was no exception. In the fall of 1867, thousands gathered on Clerkenwell Green to protest the death sentences of three Fenians in Manchester. At eight years of age, Peter didn't understand the political struggle for Ireland's independence, but he and his mates were drawn to the excitement of the huge crowd. A week before the death sentences were carried out, another man, Richard Burke, was arrested in London's Woburn Square and charged with treason. He was imprisoned at the Middlesex House of Detention in Clerkenwell, later to become the site of the Hugh Myddleton Primary School where, forty years later, Alice Geherty would attend cookery classes.

On 12 December 1867, a barrel of gunpowder was placed against the outside wall of the prison in an effort to free Burke, but it failed to ignite. A second attempt was made the following day, but by then, the prisoner had been secretly moved to another part of the prison. Apparently, the Fenian mob had little experience with explosives, because an unexpectedly massive explosion tore a sixty-foot-wide opening in the prison wall. Richard Burke would have been killed by the blast, had he not been moved. Neighbouring homes were severely damaged, and twelve area residents died in the explosion. Another forty were injured. A newspaper headline referred to the bombing as *The Clerkenwell Outrage*, a term still used to refer to the event. Support for the Fenian movement in London fell away overnight, and Thomas admonished his sons to have nothing whatsoever to do with the Fenian protests.

In 1871, when Peter was twelve-years-old, the census taker entered the word "scholar" beside his name and that of his brother, Tom. It was an important detail. In spite of their family's hardships, their generation was to become the first of the Geherty clan to read and write. Though the extent of Peter's education isn't well documented, it surely had an impact on his eventual escape from the poverty of his childhood.

Peter was dealt a final cruel blow in 1873 when his da died at the age of fifty-two. Thomas was buried unceremoniously in a common grave with several other paupers. No monument was erected to mark his final resting place. Aside from Tom and his rarely seen sister, Nell, fourteen-year-old Peter found himself alone in a predominantly Protestant, English society. With an accent more apparent than he realized, the orphaned Roman Catholic quietly endured both prejudice and indifference on his journey from boyhood to manhood. Few opportunities threw themselves at his feet.

With no one able and willing to provide for him, Peter entered St. Mary's Orphanage & Industrial School for Roman Catholic Boys on Southall Lane at North Hyde. The church-operated charity boarded in excess of 600 boys under the age of sixteen, referring to them in their records as "inmates."

There's little doubt that the youngest Geherty's childhood tested his resilience. He was well-prepared for adversity and challenge by his circumstances. It's no surprise, therefore, that his education, perseverance and hard work eventually rewarded him with a comfortable life; one the like of which his parents never dared to dream.

Peter left St. Mary's in 1875 and found work as a junior porter at The Great Northern Hotel, King's Cross Station. The hotel was established mid-century to accommodate the Great Northern Railway Company's passengers. It was one of London's earliest alternatives to the coaching inns where travellers traditionally found overnight accommodation. While Peter's income was still among the city's lowest, his position at the hotel signalled the beginning of his escape from the abject poverty of St. Luke's Parish.

When Peter's brother, Tom, married Catherine Power in November of 1880, twenty-one-year-old Peter stood alongside his sibling. At the conclusion of the ceremony, he signed his name as a witness. It was a momentous act since, only a generation earlier, his poor uneducated father, on the occasion of his *own* marriage, had signed the register with a revealing 'X'.

"Well Peter," asked Tom's bride, "is there no maiden in the whole of London whose hand you seek for yourself?"

Peter, mildly embarrassed, laughed.

"I have little to offer a wife," he replied, "though I'm treated well at the hotel, and I'm hoping for better things in years to come."

CHAPTER SIX

A CHANGE OF FORTUNE

Four months after Tom Geherty's wedding, the 1881 census described Peter as a hotel cook, one of three lodgers living with the Monard family at 18 Denmark Street, Islington. At that point, he had seen little of the world, never venturing more than a half-day's walk from the gas manufactory where his father had shovelled coal until he died. Still, Peter was curious and relied on London's newspapers to keep him informed about the world beyond the city. Stories concerning North America especially fascinated him. He read about the assassination of US President James Garfield in 1881, the Brooklyn Bridge's grand opening in 1883, and the construction of a hydro-electric plant at Niagara Falls, Canada in 1886. In 1889, *The London Gazette* reported that France's attempt to build the Panama Canal had ended in thousands of worker's deaths, most due to malaria and yellow fever. The same year, *The Illustrated London News* published detailed drawings of the newly-completed, 984-foot-high Eiffel Tower in Paris.

By the beginning of the next decade, Peter was no longer working in the hotel kitchen. He had been promoted to clerk and had received a small increase in his weekly earnings. The census listed the thirty-one-year-old bachelor as a lodger at the home of Mr and Mrs Hands on Baring Street, Shoreditch. His friends were all married with families by then, and his prospects for meeting a potential wife were limited. Then, while visiting the home of Bill Smith, an acquaintance, he was introduced to Bill's seventeen-year-old step-daughter, Rosina. Peter found the young lady attractive both in appearance and character, but he could not entertain the idea of courting one so young.

Rosina, conceived out of wedlock in Holloway, north London, had known only poverty throughout her life. Her mother, Susan, had fallen in love with a man named James Skinner. There's no record of a marriage between the two lovers, and though James was said to have been a soldier – killed before Rosina was born – her birth certificate listed his occupation as "barman." An innkeeper by the same name lived not far from Susan's humble flat on Stock Orchard Terrace, but *he* already had a wife and family.

Rosina knew nothing of her father, aside from the account she had been given by her illiterate mother, who eked out a living making artificial flowers for the millinery industry. She was barely able to support herself, let alone her child. According to census records, by the time Rosina was seven years old, she was "boarding" with the Hendley family at 17 York Buildings, St. Pancras, though in reality, little Rosina was a domestic servant, working for her meals and a dry place to sleep. From the available evidence, Rosina's early life appears to have resembled that of Charles Dickens's character, Sissy Jupe.

At age seventeen, the 1891 census described Rosina as a "domestic servant" though at that time with a butcher's family on Foxley Road, Lambeth. In the mean time, her mother married Bill Smith, and Rosina was invited to move into their house to help with the housekeeping responsibilities.

Initially, when Peter visited with the Smith family, he and Rosina exchanged little more than courteous smiles and occasional small talk.

"Hello Mr Geherty"

"Hello, Miss Skinner. I'm afraid this rain has me dripping like a park fountain."

Peter collapsed his brolly and shook the surplus water from it.

Rosina, smiling broadly, replied, "Oh, do come in out of the wet sir! Please."

Over the next few months, Peter accepted invitations to the Smith home for Sunday dinner on numerous occasions. He enjoyed the visits with the family, and Bill's wife always ensured that he had more than enough to eat. After dinner, the entire family, including Susan, their daughter, Lillian, and Rosina visited in the parlour. Bill was a reserved man and usually looked on quietly as the family shared the news of the day and the curiosities of the city with their visitor.

Over time, Bill Smith noticed that Rosina and Peter appeared particularly aware of one another's presence. Their conversations grew less formal and more substantive, and while they politely addressed everyone in the room, each appeared *most* interested in what the other had to say.

Peter, always conscious of his responsibility to his employer, never stayed late at the Smith residence. It was his habit to rise early each morning, walk thirty-five minutes to the hotel, and take up his position at the front desk on time – without fail. There he greeted patrons, checked out those who were vacating their rooms, and responded to the varied needs of the hotel's guests throughout the day. He enjoyed interacting with the customers, many of whom came from exotic places around the world, especially those who were visiting from America.

In the interim, Ellen Darcy, with whom Peter had shared the secrets and adventures of childhood, married, started a family, and emigrated to America. From time to time, the Darcy family shared snippets of her life on the other side of the Atlantic. Most often, the news was limited to the birth of a child or an illness in the family – not much else. Peter, who had few close relationships aside from Bill Smith and his family, missed his childhood friend, Ellen.

In the spring of 1893, Ellen Darcy's newly married cousin, Finn, committed to following her example by seeking a better life in the New World.

"Why don't you sail with us, Peter?" enticed Finn's wife Brigid.

"Oh, I'm not suited for farming," protested Peter.

"Bejabbers! You don't have to be a pioneer," laughed Finn, "We're going to Brooklyn, across the East River from New York City. That's where Ellen and James are; in Bay Ridge. Ellen says there's plenty of work for them that wants it."

At first, thirty-three-year-old Peter rejected the idea of leaving the city that had shaped him, but as time passed, the stories of opportunity gnawed at his resolve. In the end, he succumbed to the appeal of the adventure.

July 7, 1893, dawned cool and windy. Peter huddled beneath a nondescript brolly behind Brigid and Finn. Ahead of the trio, on the Royal Albert Dock, a line of travellers shuffled impatiently toward the S.S. *Persian Monarch*. Low, scudding clouds swept overhead before a brisk west wind. The lashing rain gathered at the ship's scuppers, spilling through them to the lock-water below. Peter's heart pounded in his chest as he climbed the gangplank of the iron-hulled screw-steamer. He was *actually* going to America.

"Mind your way, sir," chirped a member of the crew as Peter stepped aboard.

Built for trans-Atlantic service at Dumbarton, Scotland in 1880, the 360-foot barque carried a full press of sails augmented by a lone steam-powered engine. The vessel, operated by the Wilson-Hill Line, carried both passengers and cargo between London and New York. With its holds crammed with baled wool, tinplate and scotch whiskey, the 3,700-ton steamer eased through the tidal lock into the ebbing Thames. Within minutes, the ship was speeding down river before the breeze on the outgoing tide. By the time the Southend Pier came into view, North Sea swells had begun lifting her hull in a rhythmic dance familiar to its crew.

Captain Bristow squinted through the drizzle at the North Foreland Light as it slid by the starboard beam. Thirty-seven passengers were below deck, preparing to climb into their berths for the night. The rain ended while they slept, and a thick early-morning fog embraced the vessel as it entered the eastern end of the English Channel. By mid-day, the deck was awash with spray as the steam-driven barque defied a brisk west wind. Few of the passengers on board had ever been to sea, so meals were not well-attended during the first week out.

Top: S.S. Assyrian Monarch, sister-ship of the Persian Monarch.

Peter, enthralled with the romance and adventure of an ocean crossing, was not afflicted with seasickness, and spent much of each day on deck. While others were confined to their berths in agony, he stood by the rail, gazing at the turbulent seas and brooding clouds. On the third day out, he watched a distant, dark smudge on the horizon grow in size. Gradually, another steam-ship emerged beneath its own shroud of belching smoke and passed to starboard. He couldn't make out the name on its bow as the ships sailed past one another, but a crew member claimed it was the *Assyrian Monarch*, the *Persian Monarch's* sister ship.

The little vessel spent much of the first week sailing in and out of rain squalls and periods of cold dense fog. During the latter, the *Persian Monarch's* steam-powered foghorn sounded every two minutes. It was a requirement of international marine law designed to prevent collisions. Peter found it curious and somewhat entertaining that some of those on deck seemed always to be caught unawares. At two-minute intervals, in response to the sudden, penetrating blasts, many of his fellow passengers visibly jumped in unison.

On day six, a notice appeared on the daily news board requiring women and children to report to the ship's doctor in the afternoon for vaccinations. Male passengers were similarly directed to attend the following day.

During the second week of the crossing, a rumour spread quickly among passengers and crew that someone on board had died. Groups of people gathered on deck and conversed in low voices. Typhoid and smallpox outbreaks were never far from the minds of ocean-going travellers in the 19th century, but no one seemed to know anything about the deceased or the cause of death.

The following day, Captain Bristow presided over a brief ceremony, and the wrapped body of a man, whom no one seemed to remember, was consigned to the cold swells of the North Atlantic. Peter watched the canvas bundle fall and disappear with a splash. He thought about his late da.

Henry Bacon's 1879 depiction of a nineteenth-century burial at sea.

On Tuesday, the eighteenth of July, *The New York World* published a list of expected ship arrivals, including Captain Bristow's S.S. *Persian Monarch*. She was reported due to land on the twenty-first, but failed to enter the harbour until the following morning. Peter stood by the rail as usual, watching while the *Monarch* was tied to the wharf at the foot of Manhattan's Houston Street. Then he went below to collect his travelling bag. After fifteen days at sea, Peter and his fellow passengers were anxious to step ashore, but first, they had to undergo an inspection to ensure they were in good health. By late afternoon, Peter had been given clearance to enter the United States and had claimed a small trunk containing everything he owned. An hour later, he was crossing the very same Brooklyn Bridge that he had read about a decade earlier.

Peter didn't stay in America, but the reasons for his return to England are unknown. Perhaps he was homesick for London or simply disillusioned; or might he have been unable to find suitable work? Did Rosina Skinner have something to do with his change of heart?

According to a Geherty family folktale, Peter once worked aboard a ship as a steward. If, in order to pay for his return fare to England, he found a position among a ship's crew, the name "Peter Geherty" likely appears on a forgotten crew list somewhere among the dusty documents of the British National Archives.

Not long after visiting New York City, Peter returned to the city of his birth and found affordable accommodation at 11 Old Street, in the neighbourhood where he grew up. Within days, he acquired a position at the Hotel Victoria on Northumberland Avenue in Westminster.

He was still a thirty-five-minute walk away from his place of work, but he didn't mind because the hotel paid well, and the working conditions were good. The Victoria boasted 500 electrically lit guest rooms, and claimed to be the second largest hotel in London when it opened in 1887. That was the year of the queen's Golden Jubilee, and the hotel's name was a tribute to her reign. Thomas earned £2/14 a week as a clerk, performed his duties diligently, and spent as little of his wages as he could manage.

Within a few months of his brief visit to America, Peter had once again settled into an endless six-day workweek routine.

Peter and Rosina, who was then twenty-one, re-established their relationship. She found his attentions flattering. He was, in her view, a gentle-

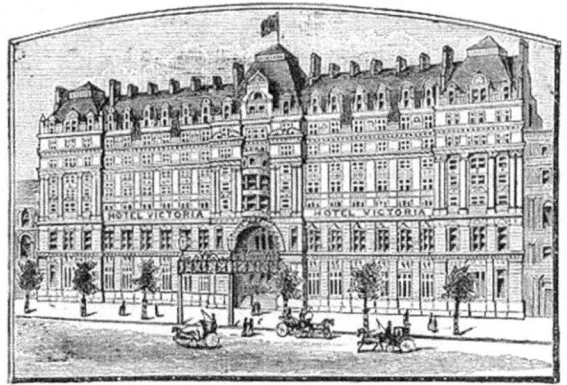

man, self assured and mature. For much of her life, she had been a domestic servant gripped by unrelenting poverty, and she found the security associated with marriage rather appealing.

In time, the couple shared short public walks, and when weather permitted, quiet conversations as they sat together on a bench in Arlington Square. Sometimes, they stood on the Islington Footpath Bridge above Regents Canal to watch the narrowboats pass below. Amid summer breezes and fluttering leaves, the couple shared their views and values, and fell in love.

Their relationship was in many ways unlikely. Peter was, after all, fourteen years older than Rosina, but more importantly, he was Roman Catholic while she belonged to the Church of England. Society considered religious affiliation an important part of life in Victorian England, and centuries of

> Alice Geherty wore a delicate gold ring on her right hand. It was set with a pair of green agates on either side of a modest Black Sea pearl. The ring had belonged to her mother, Rosina, who was said to have been a very skilled seamstress, and who had at some time prior to her marriage sewn for Princess Beatrice, Queen Victoria's youngest daughter. The princess, pleased with Rosina's work, presented her with the ring as a sign of her appreciation. It was not a particularly valuable piece of jewellery, but to Alice the ring was a precious connection to her mother and her past.

inter-religious conflict had hardened the views of families. Inter-faith marriages were uncommon and unpopular.

Nevertheless, on a warm August afternoon in 1897, Rosina and Peter were married at St. Joseph's Roman Catholic Church, Bunhill Row. It was a modest wedding with a mere handful of relatives and close friends in attendance – and no honeymoon. Instead, the couple settled into a rented flat within walking distance of the Hotel Victoria.

London, and indeed the world, had changed dramatically since Peter's father emigrated from Ireland in the autumn of 1845. Queen Victoria's empire was in the midst of celebrating her Diamond Jubilee, and the world's first horseless taxi appeared on London's streets. While it looked very similar to traditional carriages for hire, the Bersey taxi was electric.

The Victorian Era, so long associated with prosperity and scientific discovery on the one hand and filth and poverty on the other, was coming to a close. The fortunes of the Geherty family had gradually changed. Though they were far from affluent, Peter had managed to claw his way out of the degrading deprivation that his parents had once experienced. His steady employment and frugal spending practices enabled him to provide his young wife with a degree of comfort and security beyond her past life experience.

As the world hurtled toward the twentieth century, Rosina lay beside her sleeping husband in the dark. She was afraid, and yet at the same time excited, as she gently caressed her slightly rounded abdomen, feeling for signs of movement from within.

CHAPTER SEVEN

A GIFT OF STRAWBERRIES

Rosina knew when her husband would be home by looking through the window of the Geherty flat at 97 Page Street. On summer evenings, she could easily see the Great Clock at the top of Westminster's Clock Tower and watch its fourteen-foot minute hand edge toward Peter's quitting time. In the winter, when the tower was shrouded in darkness, the clock's opal glass face was backlit by a gas light. On those rare occasions, when she lost track of the time, Rosina would hear Big Ben ring out the hour – *bong, bong, bong, bong, bong, bong, bong, bong, bong* – nine times. Then she would put on the kettle for his tea, pin up her hair and listen for his footfalls on the stairs.

Peter was predictable, always on time, and his route never varied. His homeward journey began under the watchful eye of Admiral Nelson atop his 150-foot, fluted column in Trafalgar Square. From there, he passed beneath Admiralty Arch and followed The Mall to the east end of St. James Park. He especially enjoyed walking through the grassy park to Great George Street, where he turned left to Princess Street; then across Victoria to Great Smith's Street. At that point, with only four blocks to go, he quickened his pace in anticipation of a warm hug and a hot cup of tea. Invariably, Peter opened the door to his Page Street flat twenty-five minutes after setting out. It was just enough time for Rosina to prepare his supper.

Just prior to his marriage, Peter relinquished his clerk's position at The Hotel Victoria to become a dining room waiter. He enjoyed the idea of working amid the elegance of the dining room, and the position provided the Gehertys with a better income. It meant, however, that he was obliged to stay until 9 p.m. six days a week. His young bride, whom he'd nicknamed "Tommy" was happy to accommodate her husband's odd working hours. For the first time in her life, she didn't have to clean and make beds for someone else in order to survive. After putting her own little flat in order each morning, she was free to bake, sew and even read a little, now that she was married.

Rosina was excited to be living in the heart of Westminster, where she was surrounded by many of her favourite places. The Thames was two blocks away to the east, and she could walk north to Westminster and The Abbey in ten minutes. If she wished to go further afield by train or on the underground, she had only to go west to Victoria Station, a mere quarter of an hour at a comfortable pace. Even Buckingham Palace and Hyde Park were well within a casual summer Sunday stroll. The couple were content, and though Peter's income was still rather modest, the economic oppression of their respective beginnings was finally a thing of the past.

Generations of ancestors, Gehertys, Sookins, Smiths and Skinners along with scores of lesser-known surnames, came together in a moment of conception in September, 1897 – about the time that Rosina celebrated her twenty-fourth birthday. The values, traditions, language and genes of countless human beings became part of a new life. By the spring of 1898, as the birth of their first child approached, Rosina went into confinement. Her mother moved into the flat to assist with shopping, meal preparation, laundry and general housekeeping. On Thursday, the 23rd of June, the baby arrived, and the Geherty household became a popular destination for friends and family from all over Westminster and Greater London.

The proud parents named their daughter "Alice Rose" though within a short time, Peter began calling her "Queenie." He invited his colleagues at the hotel to visit, so they could meet his daughter. Many did, and one of the first, a fellow waiter, arrived when Alice was just seven days old. Being a naive bachelor, with no understanding of babies whatsoever, he puzzled over what he might bring the new-born as a gift.

"Hello Peter," he said when the flat door opened, "I've come to see baby Alice if I may."

"Of course," greeted Peter as he held out his hand, "Come in Philippe, come in!"

Philippe grasped Peter's hand and shook it vigorously, "Congratulations to you and Mrs Geherty."

Then, with a smile, he presented a small paper bag.

"For the baby," he grinned.

Because they were only briefly available in June each year, strawberries were considered a special treat, so when Philippe spied them on a vendor's cart on Horseferry Road, he didn't hesitate for a moment. It didn't occur to him that seven-day-old babies were ill equipped to eat fresh fruit, and Rosina didn't wish to offend him. To avoid embarrassing the generous young bachelor, she held a berry to little Alice's lips and allowed her to suck at it until her chin dripped with sweet, red juice. Years afterward, when all that remained of her mother were memories, Alice loved telling *the strawberry story*. Since she couldn't possibly remember the experience, her connection to the tale had undoubtedly been through her mother's account. Perhaps returning to the event enabled her, in an abstract way, to spend one more fleeting moment with her late mother.

Christened in the church where her parents were married, Alice embarked on her great adventure with enthusiasm. She was a curious child, eager to learn, and a voracious reader. She listened attentively when others spoke and weighed their words with reason and objectivity. Her mother, who was said to have frequently tired of her domestic environment, regularly insisted on moving to alternate neighbourhoods. Subsequently, Alice lived at four different addresses by the time she celebrated her third birthday. Constantly moving from one flat to another throughout her childhood provided her with a unique opportunity to become familiar with much of London. She enjoyed exploring new places and appeared to be always in search of adventure. Perhaps her deep love of the city and her adult fascination with maps was, in part, attributable to her parents. Her father, for instance, had spent much of his childhood exploring London's backwaters, while her mother seemed to harbour the restless spirit of a nomad.

When the twentieth century arrived, those who had predicted a catastrophic end to the world lost their credibility. Twenty-two days into the new century, British subjects around the world began mourning their beloved Queen Victoria. Edward VII began his reign over the British Commonwealth; the second Boer War ended, and Alice Geherty celebrated her fifth birthday at 1 Brook Street, Lambeth. Six months later, Wilbur and Orville Wright flipped a coin to see who would pilot their flying machine in what became the world's first successful powered flight. It was an historic time.

The Geherty family moved to a flat at 39 Pearman Street when Alice was six, and there in the spring of 1905, Rosina provided her daughter with a playmate, a little brother named "Arthur." Alice willingly participated in baby Arthur's care and played with him at every opportunity. Each weekday morning, she pushed her brother's pram to her primary school, kissed her mother and the baby goodbye, and went inside to learn more about the world in which she lived. Alice was driven by her need to understand and performed well for her teachers from the beginning.

Though the Geherty family moved three more times over the next two years, Alice continued to attend the same school and thoroughly enjoyed the process of learning. Among the possessions she treasured was a copy of Robert Michael Ballantyne's *The Coral Island*, presented to her in 1906 in recognition of her reading skills. She read the romantic account of castaways Ralph Rover, Jack Martin and Peterkin Gay several times and kept it for decades, eventually passing it on to one of her grandsons. Yet, the book was not her favourite. That honour went to Lewis Carroll's *Through the Looking Glass*, first published in 1871 and still popular in the first decade of the twentieth century.

Throughout much of her childhood, Alice accompanied her Roman Catholic father to Sunday services, then joined her mother in worship at the nearby Church of England. At about ten years of age, Protestantism won over her soul, and she no longer walked to mass with her father. It's possible that she simply chose the English services of her mother's church over the Catholic priests' Latin services. In any case, while her father must have been disappointed, he didn't contest her decision. Perhaps her early exposure to these disparate religious practices, which had once determined who would rule

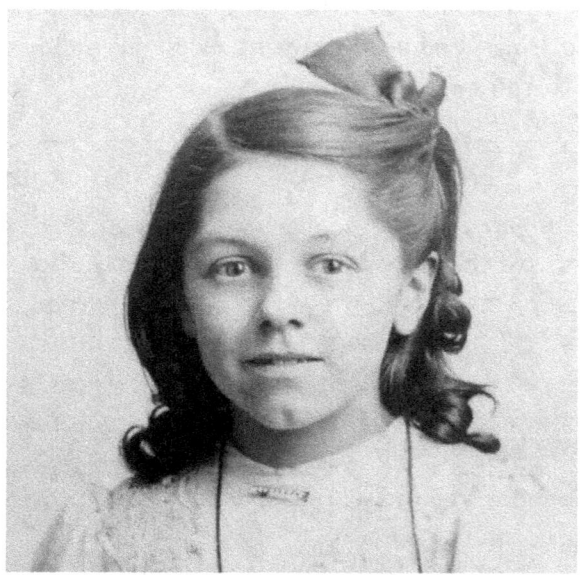

Eight-year-old Alice "Queenie" Rose Geherty

and who would be oppressed, enabled her to see both sides of other issues with calm impartiality throughout her life.

During the late nineteenth and early twentieth centuries, communication was limited almost entirely to conversation, newspapers and the Royal Mail. In fact, postal service was the *telephone* of the time. When one wished to visit a friend or relative on the other side of town, he or she would drop a postcard, announcing their intention, into the morning post, and by mid-day the addressee would have received and read the sender's message. Up to three daily deliveries throughout six days of the week provided a relatively efficient communication system within much of England and all of London.

Postcards from this period have survived at least in part because of the images they bear. Many collectors still hoard large numbers of postcards depicting hotels, seaside resorts, monuments and other popular landmarks. Others were squirrelled away in shoe boxes because of the recipient's emotional attachment to the messages they bore. Alice's summer holidays, spent with friends and relatives in Erith, Twickenham, Dover, and Southborough, may have been entirely forgotten had she not kept several postcards addressed to her at these addresses. Erith was a once popular resort town of about 30,000 residents on the south shore of the River Thames, just east of London in Kent. Alice went there on holiday in June and July of 1906. Her cousin, Kathleen, lived in Twickenham where she visited in September of 1908. She was then ten-years-old. Dover, her holiday destination in 1911, was and remains a well-known seaside resort town. Her summer holiday in Southborough, preserved in her own words, was pencilled neatly into a lined, school workbook when she was fourteen years old.

> *Two days after the school holiday commenced, I started for Southborough Kent. I arrived about 3 p.m. and after having dinner, I and my companions began to explore the place in which we meant to spend an enjoyable fortnight. On the Sunday, we went to the Church of St. Peter and St. Paul on Southborough Common. This church was a very dull looking building and had no choir. On Monday morning the weather was so bad that we could not go out, but in the afternoon the sun shone so brilliantly that we were tempted to go into the woods. So, armed with coats and rugs to sit on, we went, and took some very interesting books and some toffee. Right on the other side of the woods, between a farm*

and the woods, was a wall about five feet high; and by this wall was a ditch about ten feet wide and a mile long, all twists and turns. Here, we knew we should not be disturbed; so, we settled down for a long read until teatime. As I said before, the sun was shining beautifully, but we had not been sitting there more than half an hour when the rain began to descend heavily. We hastily gathered up our luggage & made a rush for the woods. We found a lovely spot well sheltered, and there we played "pretend" games like the little children often do, and we thoroughly enjoyed the afternoon.

On the morning of Bank Holiday, I and my two friends, Edith Allworth & Ellen Holmes walked to Leigh which is about six or seven miles from where we were staying; it was a long walk and, as we had only from 8:30 to 12:30, we had to walk pretty quickly. But as we were going along a lane one of us saw some black-berries, quite ripe. On close examination we found that some of them were an inch long. Of course, we could not pass by them, so we gathered all that we could hold and went and sat of a bank of heather close by where we could eat them. We had our hands and faces scratched and our frocks torn by the thorns, but that did not worry us. We had a curious lunch that day. Wheat, blackberries, nuts, and some "Kreamy" toffee, some of which might always have been found in our pockets – except when we had been for a walk and eaten it all. Anyhow, although the weather was bad, we spent on the whole a most enjoyable holiday.

Alice's life was undoubtedly as dissimilar to that of her ancestors as it could possibly have been.

In 1909, Alice's father obtained the position of maître d' at the Premier Hotel on Southampton Row, Russell Square. While the Premier was small compared to the 500-room Hotel Victoria, Peter's salary was substantially larger. There was, however, a difficulty to be overcome. The new workplace was a two-mile walk from the Geherty's Lambeth flat. The

Premier Hotel, 120 Southampton Row, Russell Square, London

family subsequently moved into number forty-one Granville Square, within a mile of the hotel.

London was and remains generously endowed with park-like squares. Russell Square, Berkley Square and Leicester Square, are known world-wide while others, such as Granville Square, remain quietly obscure. Surrounded on four sides by three-storey residential blocks, the square was unlikely to be accidently stumbled upon. To the residents and the congregation of the Church of St. Philip which stood in its midst when Alice was a child, the grassy, treed square formed a tranquil island of green amid the brick and stone of the world's largest city.

Alice Geherty, front row centre

Initially, Alice attended Hugh Myddelton Primary School, built in 1893 on the former site of the Clerkenwell House of Detention. 9,000 square feet of vaults dating from the prison era, and known as the Clerkenwell Catacombs, lay beneath the massive five storey building. A year later, she enrolled at Amwell Street School, only four blocks from the Geherty flat. In that year's class photo, she sat in the centre of the front row, holding a sign that read, "Amwell Street 1910."

She wore a hand-stitched, rough, woollen dress with a white lace collar. Her long dark hair was parted in the middle and pinned in place to keep it off her face. An ancient brick wall provided a backdrop for the group of ten boys and ten girls, lending an atmosphere of austerity and discipline to the scene. The children stared blankly at the camera lens, their bodies rigidly posed while the photographer implored them to remain still for a second or two. No one smiled, with a single exception; a boy immediately behind Alice who appears to have found something funny at the very moment that his image was captured.

Though a little timid at the age of twelve, Alice established a number of long-lasting relationships with her schoolmates. Among her closest friends were Nellie Marks and Connie Collier. The three girls walked to and from

> In the summer of 1908, Henry Ford's Model 'T' automobile introduced the world to a new form of personal independence. Stargazers, fascinated with the spectacle of Halley's Comet, followed its progress across the heavens through April and May of 1910. On 15 June, Captain Robert Falcon Scott embarked on his ill-fated expedition to the South Pole. In June of the following year, the coronation of King George V partially quenched Britain's obsession with ceremony and grandeur. Alice watched as history trudged on, dropping names like Albert Einstein and Theodore Roosevelt along the way.

school together, ate their lunches together, and kept in touch long after their school days came to an end.

By mid-spring, London's newspapers and Alice's school teachers were becoming increasingly preoccupied with the impending arrival of Halley's Comet. Everyone was talking about the comet's return and eagerly anticipating its arrival. Late on a relatively clear evening in mid-April, Peter took his daughter out into the chill night air to see it. They walked toward the middle of Granville Square and stood together scanning the sky.

"There Queenie," Peter urged, "there, just above the gutter on the building!"

Alice squinted into the night sky beyond her father's pointing finger, trying to discern movement among the twinkling lights above the three-storey residential structures. Just a little below Venus, the brightest "star" in the evening sky, the eleven-year-old detected a faint streak of light. It hardly seemed worthy of all the fuss, and it didn't appear to be moving in spite of the papers claims that it was streaking across the heavens at more than 120,000 miles per hour. A few alarmists had predicted the comet would cause catastrophic tidal disturbances and envelope the earth in poisonous gasses, but Peter had assured his daughter that those fears were the result of ignorance and nothing more.

The following day, Alice was fully engaged in a class discussion about comets, and sharing what she had seen from Granville Square.

At least one of Alice's school workbooks survived into the twenty-first century, providing insights into the lives of schoolchildren in 1912. While at Amwell Street School, she wrote the following descriptive account of one of her classes at Hugh Myddelton.

March 1912
Hugh Myddelton Cookery Centre
The teaching of cookery is one of the best lessons for school-girls. When I used to go to the cookery class at Hugh Middleton, I generally arrived about one minute to nine, which was nine minutes after the proper time. We all used to remain in our seats until 9.30 while our teacher marked the register, and gave instructions for the day's lessons. Then the monitors would be called to see to the two large fires, which were situated at the farther end of the room, light the gas oven, put sauce pans etc. on the stove and scrub potatoes. The dinner for the day is prepared, which consists of a dinner for six costing one shilling. As soon as the dinner is "dished up" boys come streaming in from school to buy jam tarts which are as heavy as lead, & may be bought at the rate of six for one penny. While the dinner is cooking, the teacher gives us "scullery work" to do. This is different for each girl, & she never does the same two weeks in succession. The work may be scrubbing, polishing brass, tins, knives, forks & spoons, or the fender, or cleaning the dresser, safe, or dusting & sweeping, or washing up. Then notes from the lesson are copied from the board into our notebooks, & the dinner is "dished up." Then we go home hoping mother has prepared a better dinner than we have left behind us.

The last entry in Alice's workbook was dated 3 December 1912. Eleven days later, the Christmas Holiday began, marking the end of the school term; Alice's final school term. She received recognition for her scholastic achievements in the form of a London County Council Reward Card. It came by post to her home at 8 Manchester Street, Grays Road.

Alice standing in back row, centre right.

Queenie's life was at a crossroads. No longer would she enjoy the freedom of her childhood school days with her friends. Though she was still five months away from her fifteenth birthday, it was time for her to go to work. Shortly after Christmas, in January of 1913, she found employment as a stenographer at J. Cowen and Company, a blouse manufacturer located at 4 Vestry Street, Hoxton. She worked there from 8 a.m. to 6 p.m. for a weekly salary of six shillings. Her employer's premises was almost two miles from her home, but she enjoyed the walk on clear days, and she could resort to the underground if the weather was bad.

Alice really missed her friend, Connie, when the Collier family emigrated to Canada in the summer of 1912. Still, they kept in touch by writing to one another regularly. Alice's first question after arriving home from work was often, "Was there anything in the post for me?"

Connie's letters described in detail her family's trans-Atlantic voyage, her new home on Barton Street in Hamilton, and the nearby Lake Ontario.

"It's so big it looks like a sea," wrote Connie.

Alice could hardly believe what she read when her friend described her first winter in Canada. She knew about North America's winter snow, but Connie's letter claimed the water in the city's harbour froze solid enough to support hundreds of people. It just sounded too fantastic.

Alice, who had never been out of southern England, loved reading Connie's letters and always filled her replies with questions about life in Canada. She had known her friend's parents and had met some of Connie's siblings prior to their emigration to Canada, but she never imagined that she and the Colliers would become intimately connected by a war still more than a year in her future.

By July of 1913, Alice had moved on to a job at Page & Thomas, a commercial printer of fine arts located at 131 Finsbury Pavement. She earned ten shillings per week there and remained in that position until November of 1914, by which time the Great War had begun raging across Europe.

CHAPTER EIGHT

JOSEPH'S THIRD SON

About the time that Peter Geherty returned to London from New York, a mail sorter's wife gave birth to a son at 26 Lesly Street in Islington. The infant's parents, Joseph Henry Collier and Anne Marie Noquet, were somewhat representative of the neighbourhood. Joseph was the grandson of an Irish immigrant, and Anne was the granddaughter of a Huguenot refugee, exiled from France by the intolerance of French Catholicism. They and their neighbours endured their lives with little enthusiasm, and in that they were justified.

From without, the terraced houses of both sides of Lesly Street resembled three-storey, pale yellow, brick walls with entrances at intervals of twelve feet. Windows of modest design and size invited London's dim urban daylight into dull rented flats. Behind each window, worn parlour furniture and ragged carpets huddled around smoky hearths. The train of nondescript addresses, seamlessly joined one to the next, filled the entire length of the one-block street. Its residents, struggling to provide for their families, plodded dutifully to and from their places of work six days out of seven. Just two short blocks away, the walls of the fifty-year-old Pentonville Prison threatened those who were tempted to improve their lot through crime. Beyond the prison, the Metropolitan Cattle Market's slaughter house polluted the air with the stench of death, while the coal yards of the Great Northern Railway disbursed a fine black dust. Lesly Street was hardly a neighbourhood of choice.

Joseph's third son, John Albert, was destined to be known to his friends and family as 'Jack'.

Though another brother and two sisters came after him, he was always the runt of the family, a mere five-foot-five and 125 pounds at the age of twenty-one. Born in the fall of 1894, the year that London's Tower Bridge was opened and bottles of Coca Cola first went on sale in America, he witnessed some of history's greatest moments.

As a small boy, Jack moved along with his family to 85 Trumpington Road, Forest Gate. There, he and his brothers attended Cann Hall Road

> Details may seem pointless at times, but they often tell a story that might otherwise go unnoticed. Is it inconsequential that Jack's middle name was Albert? None of his known ancestors bore that name. Was it simply the random choice of his parents? In reality, the Colliers, like many Britons at the time, revered their Queen and her consort, Prince Albert. The prince was enormously popular with the people, and his name became rather fashionable in the late nineteenth century. John Albert Collier was just one of thousands of newborns who bore the name "Albert" in the late Victorian period.

School and spent their Sunday mornings in St. Margaret's Church, which boasted pews capable of accommodating 800 parishioners.

The Collier boys were not, however, angels. Their propensity for mischief was well known in the neighbourhood, and it was rumoured that they sometimes blamed their transgressions on another family of Colliers who lived nearby.

John (Jack) Collier, front row, second from left.

On leaving school in 1909, fourteen-year-old Jack earned £1/7s/3d a week as a shop assistant, but he didn't stay at that job for long. Adventure and opportunity awaited him on the other side of the Atlantic. His brothers, Joe and Frank, had already emigrated to Canada where they were hard at work on the Frances farm near Georgetown, Ontario. Every penny they could spare was set aside for Jack's passage to Canada. Mr Frances had agreed to employ him on the farm for a couple of months until he found work elsewhere. Then, with three incomes, the Collier boys hoped to save enough to bring their parents, sisters and younger brother to Canada as well.

Joe Collier was quiet, mature, compact and steady; a young man who preferred to go unnoticed. His brother, Frank, was outgoing, tall and good-looking; a clever, take-charge sort of fellow. Their little brother was tough, wiry, and quick in both mind and body. He had more than his fair share of raw courage, and he was to have many opportunities to prove it.

Jack's mother packed his things and served him a hearty breakfast before accompanying him to Leytonstone Station. His sisters, twelve-year-old Constance and seven-year-old Violet, followed behind, holding hands with one another and skipping much of the way. The girls were chatty and competed for their brother's attention as they bounced along the footway toward the station. Mrs Collier was unusually quiet. She was reliving a similar farewell when Joe and Frank had set out two years earlier. Joe's letters had been reassuring and hopeful. He and Frank enjoyed living and working on the Frances farm, and they were being well-fed. Could a mother hope for anything more? Still, it was hard to see another son leave, even with her husband's assurance that the rest of the family would soon join them in Canada.

No tears were shed, though Jack's eyes seemed to glisten a little more than usual. Anne was deliberately stoic, and the girls, excited about their big brother's pending adventure, had not given much thought to how long it would be before they saw him again. The four hurried onto the platform amid clouds of hissing steam. Anne kissed Jack goodbye as if he would return on the evening train. The massive black locomotive and its sooty coal tender seemed eager to get underway. A circular corporate emblem on its side declared "The London and North-Western Railway" in white enamel paint.

Jack, a full five months short of his sixteenth birthday, lugged his suitcase toward a passenger coach and stepped aboard without looking back. He wiped his eyes discretely as he made his way to the nearest vacant seat, then waved cheerily from the open window. The train lurched in the direction of Euston Station, while the young Collier boy slumped onto the seat by the window and stared blankly at the empty seat beyond his knees.

Jack barely heard the rattles, clicks and bangs as the passenger coach sped on its way toward Liverpool. He was both enthusiastic to see America and reluctant to leave home; excited about his future, yet anxious about facing the unknown; confident in his own abilities but unsure of what to expect. His head was swimming; his mind, numb. The family had discussed his journey over dinner on many occasions, and Jack's father had prepared him as best he could, but the enormity of the undertaking had escaped him until the train had begun to move. After a while he slept, then peered out at the speeding landscape for a while – then slept again.

Throughout the day, Jack watched his fellow travellers board and disembark at Bletchley, Roade, Rugby, Nuneaton, Litchfield, Stafford and Crewe. Most passengers stared vacantly through the windows or read their newspapers in silence, avoiding eye contact with one another.

Even the conductor addressed no one in particular when he called "Tickets, please!"

The man took Jack's ticket, punched it and handed it back without a word. A few minutes earlier, Jack had been a celebrity of sorts in the eyes of his sisters. Then suddenly, he felt invisible and was momentarily afflicted with an unfamiliar feeling; loneliness.

When he arrived at the Liverpool Exchange Station, he was met by a representative of the Salvation Army and escorted to the Liverpool Landing Stage where the ship was moored. He could barely believe his eyes when he saw the vessel up close for the first time. He'd seen ships in the Thames River from a distance, but none had compared with the iron monster looming above the wharf. *How could such a behemoth possibly float*, he wondered?

Jack, in the midst of a long line of passengers, shuffled toward the boarding ramp of the S. S. *Laurentic*. At the top of a newspaper, tucked under the arm of a man ahead of him, he read "Saturday, May 28, 1910". The air was cold and the sky was obscured by dirty, swiftly moving clouds. They were coming from the west – *from Canada*. He shifted the heavy suitcase to his other hand and wondered if the weather was warm in Georgetown.

"Fifteen," Jack answered when the purser asked his age; "ten dollars," when asked how much money he had. The word sounded strange.

"Dol-lars," he repeated.

"What will your occupation be in Canada lad?"

"I'm going to work on a farm with my brothers," he replied proudly.

A few minutes later, Jack found himself deep inside the ship among his fellow third-class passengers, all of whom were hoping to find a better life at the end of the voyage.

Young Jack sailed out of Liverpool aboard the Canadian-Pacific Service's largest vessel, the 15,000-ton S.S. *Laurentic*. The liner's lone black and vermillion funnel sparkled with newness. She had been launched less than two years earlier at Belfast and had sailed from Liverpool to Quebec on her maiden voyage the previous April. Jack was one of 1,617 passengers aboard, but he was special; he was the youngest unaccompanied male on the ship.

Master Collier's name, hand-written in the ship's manifest, was closely followed by the faint impression of a stamp that read, "Salvation Army." At the time, charitable institutions such as the Salvation Army offered assistance to working class emigrants in an effort to reduce the number of poor in London. Australia and Canada were recommended destinations.

There were no storms to brand the passage heroic and only a few distant icebergs were seen as the vessel skirted Newfoundland and entered the Strait of Belle Isle. The *Titanic*, anonymous to all but those involved in her construction, was still a year from being launched. Throughout the eight-day passage, the *Laurentic*'s rail defined young Collier's world, but he did his best to explore every accessible inch of the 565-foot-long ship. He even managed a brief peek into the first-class smoking and reading room, where to his amazement, copious rays of sunlight poured in through skylights high above his upturned face. He never managed to breach the sanctity of the first-class dining room where bacon was served for breakfast, though he enjoyed the lingering smell of it in the corridors every morning.

Most days, Jack filled his belly with oatmeal or shredded wheat at breakfast as did the majority of the third-class passengers. Mid-day meals and suppers were equally bland though the tea was plentiful and generally hot enough to be enjoyed after his meal with a scone or a custard.

While excited by the wonders of the ship and the prospect of finding adventure in Canada, Jack felt very small and vulnerable in his berth at the end of the day. He missed his home, his family, and London, and he was eager to see his brothers and the end of his journey.

The frigid Labrador Current embraced the single-funnelled Laurentic as she entered the Gulf of St. Lawrence. Though it was then June, it felt like February to her English passengers. The current's cold water sucked the spring warmth from the air and chilled the ship's hull. When the vessel reached the north shore settlement of Cap à l'Aigle, ninety miles from the city of Quebec, the icy upwelling current joined the river's out-flow on the surface and returned to the Atlantic. Almost immediately, the air took on the feel of spring, and the mood aboard the ship changed.

S.S. Laurentic *(R.M.S.* Laurentic *when its steamship designation changed to "Royal Mail Ship")*

The *Laurentic*'s massive steel hull thumped against the wharf at Quebec City on the morning of June the 4th. Its crew ushered the passengers into the arms of doctors and customs officials. The same series of questions was directed to each of the disoriented passengers as they muddled through the bureaucratic landing process.

The Chateau Frontenac, built seventeen years earlier by Canadian Pacific Railway, towered over Jack and his inquisitors. He hadn't expected to see such an imposing presence in the colony.

By midday, Jack found himself on the dock lugging a suitcase which his uncle Jim had given him for the trip. It was constructed of wood and sheathed in leather that must have once been almost orange in colour. Its finish was, by that June afternoon, dulled by a lifetime of bruises and scuffs. Two leather straps encircled its girth as if it would burst without them. Jack hefted the unwieldy suitcase and allowed himself to be swept along the dock in a current of strangers moving toward the city. Finding his way to the nearby train station wasn't difficult, but the French language notices and signs made locating the Toronto-bound platform a little tricky. Steam hissed, bells clanged, and the metallic thump of couplings echoed throughout the station. Burgundy coloured Canadian Pacific Railway coaches, much larger than their European counterparts, awaited shouts of "all aboard." Street-wise from growing up in north-east London, Jack soon overcame his confusion and found himself boarding a C.P.R. passenger coach. He pushed his battered suitcase onto a slatted rack above an empty seat and sat by the window beneath it. The carriage was cold, and the seat was hard.

It didn't seem long before the train reached Toronto where Jack's oldest brother, Joe, was waiting for him to step from the train.

"Jack! Jack Collier!" called Joe.

Jack spun around, banging the cumbersome suitcase against his shin.

"Joe!" he cried, and his voice cracked.

The elder brother was not the boy that Jack remembered; he was a man. Jack hardly managed two steps with his heavy burden before Joe wrapped him roughly in a rowdy hug. The bag dropped heavily onto the platform as the siblings embraced one another. They walked through Toronto's Union Station to the Grand Trunk platform to board the train to Georgetown, while exchanging the latest family news. Joe inquired about their sisters, and Jack described his Atlantic crossing.

"Did you see any icebergs?" prodded Joe.

"A few," Jack responded, "but they were rather far away – a mile or so I'd guess. One of the passengers, an old German man, let me look through his field glasses. I could see swirls of green in the ice. I wish we'd been closer."

Grand Trunk Railway Station, Georgetown, 1908

A couple of hours later, Jack found himself just west of Georgetown, sitting at the Frances family's dinner table. The windows were open, and a summer breeze was playing with the curtains. Cutlery clicked, rattled and scraped against china while everyone asked questions about England and the *Laurentic*. They listened attentively to Jack's responses while passing bowls and plates of vegetables and meat around and across the table. The house was warm and comfortable, and the family were behaving as if he was a long-lost relative. Living in Canada had always appealed to him, but until that meal, vague unspoken doubts had lingered behind his dreams.

Imperceptibly over several months, the centre of Jack's reality shifted from London to Georgetown. The Collier boys enjoyed their time on the farm. The work was hard, and the hours were long, but Mr and Mrs Frances were more like family than employers, and they treated the boys like their own. On weekends, and occasionally on an errand to fetch something from Willoughby's General Store, Jack would go into Georgetown. It wasn't very big, just one street of shops and a few warehouses, mills and factories, but he enjoyed it just the same. He often found himself on the iron bridge that crossed the Credit River near John Barber's Paper Mill. Sometimes he and the Frances boys would dig worms for bait, and hang their fishing poles over the river there on a Sunday afternoon.

There were few opportunities for recreation when harvest time arrived. In fact, the boys worked from dawn to dusk. The only time they weren't working was when they were snoring in their beds or eating a meal at the Frances family's kitchen table. Jack had never seen so much food on one table before, and he ate like a horse; at least, that's what Mrs Frances said.

As the harvest season slowed, Mr Frances asked Jack to come with him into the barn for a minute.

"You're a good worker, Jack," the farmer began, "You work hard and don't complain. I like that, but the winter's coming, and I don't have enough work to keep you on."

"That's all right, Mr Frances," Jack responded, "Joe told me I'd only be able to work here for a while."

"Okay son, so you understand that I'd keep you on if I could?"

"Oh sure, Mr Frances."

"You can live here until you find work. I won't just throw you out!" he laughed.

"Can I take the buggy into town on Monday?" Jack asked.

"Okay, be careful crossing the bridge. Sammy gets spooked when the wheels hit those planks," said Mr Frances as he turned to leave.

After taking a step toward the door, he stopped, turned back, and looked at Jack.

"How old are you, Jack?" he asked.

"Fifteen, but I'll be sixteen October thirty-first!"

"You're not very big. It might be hard to get a full-time job until then," he said thoughtfully.

The following morning, Jack hitched Sammy to the buggy and followed the Guelph Road to Georgetown. By lunch time he was feeling a little discouraged, but Mr MacKenzie at the lumber yard had suggested he apply at the glove factory.

"I heard they're lookin' for men there," he said.

Jack had picked an apple as he walked by the tree on his way to the barn that morning, and Mrs Frances had made him a cheese sandwich to take for lunch. He sat in the buggy just outside the lumber yard while he ate the sandwich. Then he ate half of the apple and fed the rest to Sammy before making his way to the glove factory at the corner of Guelph and Water Streets. He stepped down from the buggy and stood looking up at the three-storey brick building for a minute before pushing the door open and going inside.

"What was your last job?" asked Mr Arnold.

"I work on the Frances farm, sir, haying and picking, and tending the livestock, sir."

"Still there?" asked the man.

"Yes sir, but there won't be much to do there in the winter, sir."

"How old are you?"

The words startled Jack. He knew they were coming, but he wasn't as ready for them as he thought he was. He could feel the blood rushing to his face. "I'm sixteen," he lied.

Mr Arnold tilted his head to one side and eyed Jack up and down. "Sixteen? When was your birthday?"

"August thirty-first," Jack offered as he glanced out the window of Mr Arnold's office.

Mr Arnold, who had been standing over Jack in front of his desk, adjusted his tie, thrust one hand into his pants pocket and walked behind his desk. He slumped into his chair heavily.

"Alright. Come back next Monday at seven sharp and see Mr Byford. He'll get you started."

Jack thanked the company's founder enthusiastically and hurried home to tell everyone he had obtained a job in the glove factory. He had no idea what he would be doing, and he didn't actually know yet how much he was going to be paid, but he had a job!

H. T. Arnold & Sons Glove Factory produced gloves and mitts of sheepskin, dog skin, pigskin, calfskin, horsehide and buckskin. Jack apparently proved to be a conscientious worker, eager to learn new skills, because he was soon assigned to the role of a glove cutter under the supervision of Frank Byford. Like the other forty employees at the factory, he worked fifty-nine hours a week and received fifteen cents per hour which amounted to $8.85 weekly. The company produced almost 900 pairs of gloves daily and sold them all over eastern Canada.

Though Jack enjoyed living on the Frances farm, he had to find accommodation nearer his place of work, so when Frank Byford offered his young apprentice a room in his Georgetown home, Jack accepted without hesitation. Frank's wife Dora fed him, did his laundry and occasionally cleaned his room, and Jack remained a lodger at the Byford house at 89 Main Street until his parents arrived from England in 1912.

The skills Jack learned at the glove manufactory, proved advantageous when he moved to Hamilton in 1912, and again almost a decade later, when he returned along with thousands of others from the Great War.

By the end of October 1910, the rush to bring in the crops and prepare for spring planting on the Frances farm was winding down. The daylight hours were getting shorter, and while countless maintenance tasks had yet to be dealt with, Ontario winters were long and there would be time enough before spring arrived. Jack was often invited to visit his brothers and the Frances family on Sundays and sometimes stayed for dinner. Sunday, October 30th was one of those occasions. When the men came into the kitchen for supper, they found the table filled with an assortment of meats and vegetables as usual, but the atmosphere seemed different to Jack. The conversation was a little less natural in some way, and Jack noticed the others were exchanging looks periodically without speaking. He felt some sort of private joke was being kept from him. When everyone's plate was scraped clean, Mrs Frances served steaming cups of tea all around before retreating into the kitchen again. Then, she returned with a cake, and everyone broke into a hearty rendition of *For He's a Jolly Good Fellow*. Jack blushed with embarrassment. Mr Frances had remembered their discussion in the barn a couple of weeks earlier. Jack turned sixteen years old at midnight.

> At 2:20 a.m. on the 15th of April, 1912, after striking an iceberg at latitude 41° 43' 37" North and longitude 49° 56' 54" West, the "unsinkable" R.M.S. *Titanic* sank in more than 12,000 feet of water. A mere thirty-seven seconds elapsed between the lookout's first glimpse of the iceberg and the collision that shocked the world's mariners and travellers alike. In all, 1,495 men, women and children died in the frigid North Atlantic that night.

On the 16th of July, 1912, Jack's parents and their three youngest children rode an early morning train to Southampton and boarded the Quebec-bound S.S. *Ascania*. Outwardly, Joseph was relaxed about his family's voyage to Canada, but secretly, he shared their apprehension at the prospect of sailing across the North Atlantic. It was a warm summer day on England's south coast, but he knew that icebergs lurked in the frigid waters off Newfoundland well into summer. Besides, there were other dangers. Ship collisions were not uncommon along the fog-bound coast, and the Atlantic storms were legendary. The *Titanic* disaster had proven that no ship was unsinkable, and every crossing was dangerous regardless of the shipping lines' claims.

In 1911, the city of Hamilton, located at the west end of Lake Ontario, was growing faster than any other North American city, in part because it was located at the junction of two railways. That, and the fact that it had a large landlocked harbour, was attracting industry at an unprecedented rate. The details of Joseph and Anne Collier's arrival in Canada, along with how and why they came to live in Hamilton, have been lost to time, but plentiful jobs were undoubtedly a factor. They initially rented a house from James Perry at 626 Barton Street, East in late 1912. There, the entire family of eight was reunited under one roof. Jack left his job at the Georgetown glove factory and went to work for Edwin W. Toll, the proprietor of the Hamilton Glove Works at 158 Wellington Street, South.

Joseph Senior didn't stay at his Hamilton address long. Instead, he signed onto a railway construction crew, bid his family goodbye, and headed west to earn a living in Prince George, British Columbia. It seems an odd choice of occupations given his past work experience as a mail sorter in England, but perhaps his options were limited, and his need for an above average income was acute. 2,500 miles from Hamilton, at a construction camp on the Fraser River, Joseph operated a *donkey* engine, a small locomotive used to move men and equipment in rail yards and along rail lines under construction. He also served as a cook to the other workers. A few months later, he returned to his family with all but a few dollars of his earnings intact.

CHAPTER NINE

THE COMING TOGETHER

*572 Wentworth Street North, Hamilton, Ontario (left),
as it appeared a century later*

In 1914, Joseph acquired a recently built house at 572 Wentworth Street North, where he and his wife lived until 1923. Jack lived there too until he went to war in 1915.

As the second decade of the twentieth century unfolded, nationalist sentiments, territorial disputes, and memories of past conflicts fuelled tensions among the states of Europe. By the spring of 1914, international paranoia was spreading like a plague throughout the continent. Then, on June 28, assassin Gavrilo Princip pulled the trigger of his .038 calibre pistol in Sarajevo, and Archduke Franz Ferdinand lay dead. The political consequences were enormous. Immediately, a complex system of international alliances began dragging one nation after another into the worldwide conflict known as the Great War.

Nations aligned themselves with one side or the other. Germany declared war on France, sending troops and materiel through Belgium, a neutral nation allied with Britain. On August 4, the lives of British citizens throughout the world changed when the British Cabinet resolved to go to war with the German aggressors.

Britain declared war on Germany on August 4, 1914. Alice, then sixteen years old, was unable to fully comprehend what war would mean to her and her family. She had been helping her mother pack their things in preparation for yet another move; this time to number 6 Bond Street, Holford Square. The family's change of address, the week after England entered the war, occupied her thoughts and daily life for a while. The newspaper headlines addressed events and political issues that Alice deemed distant and irrelevant. She had no inkling of the changes the world-wide conflict would bring over the next six years. She couldn't even begin to imagine them, but Alice in London and Jack Collier in Canada were affected in ways that would dramatically change their lives forever.

By the end of 1914, most the world's powerful nations were sending their young men into battle. The German navy began shelling targets along the coasts of England, and the first bomb was dropped on Dover from a German airship. Once more, the Geherty family moved; this time to 100 Cloudesley Road, Highbury.

Canada, a dominion of the British Empire, was automatically and immediately committed to the conflict. Canada's Governor General, His Royal Highness the Duke of Connaught, announced that the Dominion was at war. Support for Britain's conflict was widespread within Canada's Anglo-Saxon population, and the Colliers were no exception.

In the pre-radio society of 1914, the news reached 572 Wentworth Street through the excited shouts of neighbours who had seen the headlines in the Hamilton Herald. The Collier boys quickly expressed their eagerness to defend England against the Huns. Their mother, though herself strong-willed, self-assured and loyal to her homeland, was frightened by the prospect of her sons stepping onto a battlefield. Joseph, like many, believed the war would be a short one, and he encouraged his boys to wait to see how events developed.

Though barely aware of one another's existence, a complex web of circumstances was quietly at work putting Jack Collier and Alice Geherty on intersecting paths toward a shared story of war, romance, love and adventure.

Joe, the first of the three Collier brothers to volunteer for the Canadian Expeditionary Force, enlisted on the 11th of November. Suddenly, the Collier family's future became unpredictable and permeated with unspoken fears. Across the Atlantic, Alice's father, Peter, was fifty-five years old, and her brother, Arthur, had not yet celebrated his tenth birthday. Subsequently, the Geherty family was spared much of the anxiety associated with going to war.

Two years after Alice Geherty's birth, in the summer of 1900, a hydrogen-filled airship designed by Count Ferdinand Zeppelin soared into the sky above Germany. The cumbersome, cigar-shaped invention attracted a lot of attention, but its practical value wasn't fully appreciated at the time. The success of its flights depended on near-perfect weather conditions, and only thrill-seeking adventurers were willing to go aloft, even on the finest of days. Over time, however, Zeppelin technology improved until a decade and a half later, German airships attacked Norfolk, England in the Great War's first air raid on Britain. Though seen as unwieldy 600-foot-long targets, they were capable of speeds approaching eighty-five miles per hour, and they could reach altitudes of up to 14,000 feet. In addition to five defensive machine guns and a crew of twenty, German Zeppelins carried more than 4,400 pounds of bombs.

By the spring of 1915, Alice was employed as a clerk at a builders' supply, T. Ide & Company at 32 Rathbone Place, where her weekly salary had grown to fifteen shillings. Until then, her life had not been greatly impacted by the war. On the 31st of May, three weeks prior to her seventeenth birthday, that changed. Twenty-eight Londoners were reported killed that day when bombs were dropped on the city from above. Suddenly, the war was real. No longer was it confined to the black and white text and images in *The London Illustrated News*. In a single night, Alice's comfortable world disintegrated.

"I remember telling my mum a couple of times that the war frightened me, and she always scoffed and said I shouldn't worry myself. Then, the day after those people were killed, I was getting ready for work, and Mum said I should go into the Tottenham Court Road Station if there was a raid. I realized at once that Mum was afraid too."

England gathered her brave young men from every corner of the empire. The distant war offered young Canadian men adventure and an opportunity to demonstrate their patriotism and courage. It aroused a latent sense of duty and honour instilled by their families and the post-Victorian culture of the time. Union Jacks were everywhere, and recruiting posters carried messages such as, "Here's your chance. It's <u>MEN</u> we want!"

Jack told his parents and Mr Toll at the Hamilton Glove Works that he was going to volunteer for overseas service. Neither his parents nor his employer wanted him to go, but neither would they insist he stay. It was his duty, and as patriots of The British Empire they accepted his enlistment as inevitable. In early February of 1915, he joined a local militia known as the 1st Field Troop, Canadian Engineers and began training for war. At the time, Jack had no way of knowing that his unit wouldn't be sent to Europe, but the Federal Government ultimately decided that its militias would not be mobilized. Rather, it planned to raise a separate, voluntary Canadian Expeditionary Force.

In response to the need for a diversified Canadian Expeditionary Force, the 86th Machine Gun Battalion, the first of its kind in the British Empire, was raised at Hamilton in mid-August 1915. Lieutenant Colonel Walter Wilson Stewart, along with the battalion's officers, began hand-picking personnel from local militia units. Only men who met their high standards were chosen. The 1st Field Troop Engineers was one of those militias, and Jack Collier was among the young men selected. He signed his Attestation Paper on the 18th of August and was assigned to the battalion's 'B' Company under Major Gordon Ferrie.

In little more than a week, the 86th Battalion grew to 600 men, and by Septem-

1915 Hamilton Area Recruiting Poster

ber 23rd when it departed for training at Camp Niagara, it was a thousand strong. The battalion remained in Niagara for more than a month, but no machine guns were yet available. Instead, the recruits were issued rifles and underwent standard infantry training.

Upon returning to Hamilton on November 9, the new unit was stationed at the recently renovated Armouries on James Street North. The men were kept busy with lectures, drills and route marches into Hamilton's outlying areas. In March of 1916, the 86th Battalion was issued machine guns, and the men began their training in earnest.

1,000-strong 86th Machine Gun Battalion on parade at Camp Niagara in the summer of 1915

The Canadian military adopted the British Army's Maxim Machine Gun. It was manufactured by Vickers Limited of England, and was considered superior to all other contemporary machine guns. Still, it had its drawbacks. The gun, along with its detachable tripod, weighed seventy-eight pounds and required a crew of five or six men to keep the weapon operational in the field. Three carried several twenty-two-pound belts of .303 calibre ammunition, essential to the weapon's operation. During continuous fire, the gun gobbled up more than 450 rounds per minute. The other three men were known as "Number One," "Number Two" and "Number Three."

In combat, Jack Collier was a Number One. It was his job to carry the fifty-pound tripod and place it in the precise position from which he intended to fire the gun. Number Two's responsibility was to carry the twenty-eight-pound gun, which contained an additional nine pounds of water in the barrel's cooling jacket, and place it on the tripod while Jack locked the two together. The man designated as "Number Three" carried a canvas belt of ammunition, which Number Two fed into the gun while it was being locked onto the tripod. Jack then cocked the weapon, pulled the belt through, and began firing. The drill was practiced repeatedly until every member of the team performed flawlessly. Then they practiced some more.

When Jack and his comrades were granted a three-day pass in the spring of 1916, they sensed something was up. Rumours spread like a prairie fire through the excited battalion. Jack went home and told his family that he would be going to England within days though he didn't know any details. His mother prepared a meal reminiscent of a Christmas feast and forbade anyone from talking about the war at the table. Her eldest boy was already overseas, and she would not have her remaining children see her cry. Jack made a promise to write at every opportunity.

A few days later, immediately following a scheduled kit inspection, the spit and polish recruits were marched to Hamilton's Grand Trunk Station and packed into carriages for their journey to Canada's east coast. Hundreds of well-wishers stood cheering on the embankment overlooking the tracks. Men held their hats above their heads, while mothers, wives and sisters waved white handkerchiefs as the battalion boarded the train in khaki battle dress. White steam hissed, and black smoke belched, as the massive iron engine lurched into motion. Jack settled onto a wooden bench for the long ride, made even longer by numerous stops along the route. Frequently, the train halted to take on water, connect to additional carriages, and welcome Canada's eager sons aboard. Jack had lost count of the stops by the time he fell asleep in Rivière-du-Loup. He and his boisterous comrades had been, at first, far too excited to sleep, but no one could last forever.

When Jack awoke, he peered through the carriage's rain-streaked window at unfamiliar buildings, between which a ship's twin funnels could be seen. The cream-coloured stacks were topped with wide black bands.

"Where are we?" he asked no one in particular.

"Halifax," responded Sergeant Clark from across the aisle.

The khaki-clad 86th Battalion was detrained at Halifax's North Street Station and marched in full kit to the nearby docks. There, the British 20,000-ton S.S. *Adriatic* waited amid a flurry of activity. Built a decade earlier by Harland and Wolff of Belfast, the ship had sailed to the Empire's western colony to fetch its fittest and gamest young warriors, many of whom were destined to spend eternity in French graves.

At the time, the S.S. *Adriatic* was among the fastest British ships ever built, and perhaps because of that, managed to survive the Great War intact.

S.S. Adriatic *in Belfast, Ireland, prior to her sea trials.*

She sailed out of Halifax Harbour with her precious cargo of cannon fodder on May 19, 1916. A ship's officer later referred to the crossing as "a dirty one," with several hundred young men seasick for most of the ten-day crossing. On May 22, while still at sea, the 86th Machine Gun Battalion was re-designated the Canadian Machine Gun Depot (CMGD).

The fresh troops disembarked at Liverpool on the 29th of May and formed up on the wharf to await a kit inspection. An Irish Sea drizzle dripped from the peaks of their forage caps as they stood at attention with their backs to the *Adriatic*'s hull. Lieutenant-Colonel Stewart and a contingent of British Army Officers passed slowly before the ranks of Canadian soldiers.

Then, "Baaa ... Taaal ... **YUN!**"

A thousand volunteers stood tense, awaiting the command.

"Laayefff ... ***TURN!***"

Each young man, eyes fixed on an imaginary point somewhere in front of his face, pivoted on his left heel in unison, lifted his right foot and slammed it down onto the wharf. The sound of a thousand leather soles striking wet tarmac was impressive. Again, rigid and staring straight ahead with their shoulders back, they waited.

"By the left, ... qui ... ick ... ***March!***"

The 86th Battalion stepped off proudly in the direction of the Liverpool Exchange railway station. Loaded yet again onto Spartan railway carriages, the men embarked on a 300-mile journey to Folkestone in Kent.

The sun set prior to the battalion's arrival, so Jack saw little more than shadows and the glow of gas lights as he and his comrades were paraded and loaded onto lorries for the short drive to Shorncliffe Army Camp. There, at Risborough Barracks they were assigned to bunks in two-storey brick buildings on either side of Pond Hill Road. Jack was impressed. He had expected to be quartered in eight-man tents like those in Camp Niagara, or draughty wooden H-huts at best. He wrote his mother, expounding the virtues of the luxury accommodations.

The men of the Canadian Machine Gun Depot were destined to remain at Shorncliffe for eighteen weeks of drill, inspections and additional weapons training. They were paid at the rate of a dollar a day while posted overseas, about thirty-five cents a day less than a factory worker back in Canada. Shortly after his arrival in England, Jack assigned fifteen dollars of each month's pay to his father in Canada. The remaining fifteen or sixteen dollars was sufficient to provide for his personal needs and fund a visit to London now and then.

Canadian soldiers were allotted six days leave on arrival in Britain, but leaves were usually limited to two days at a time, taken on weekends so as not to interfere with training schedules. In addition, only twenty per cent of the unit were allowed leave at one time. Jack's first opportunity came on the 24th of June, when he was granted his first leave of 1916. In reality, because the pass didn't allow him to leave the camp until 1 p.m. on Saturday and required him to return by midnight Sunday, his leave was more like a day and a half. Still, he'd been looking forward to seeing the city of his boyhood for some time, and he didn't lose a minute getting to the station to catch a train to London.

Jack's sister, Connie, had been regularly corresponding with Nellie Marks, one of her London schoolmates, since the Collier family emigrated to Canada. She suggested Nellie meet Jack when he got leave to go to London.

"I'm sure he'll appreciate your company," she wrote.

Jack remembered Nellie, but he was fifteen when he last saw her, and she was then only twelve years old. As agreed, he sent her a postcard to advise that he would meet her at the Ferringdon Street underground station, and Nellie, being somewhat anxious about the meeting, invited her best friend, Alice Geherty, to come along. Eighteen-year-old Alice, another of Connie's classmates, only vaguely remembered the Collier boys from her primary school days and wasn't sure if she had met Jack.

"Which one is Jack?" queried Alice as they approached the station.

"He's the second youngest of the brothers. You remember," coaxed Nellie, "the little one."

"Was he the boy that went to Canada a couple of years before Connie?" asked Alice.

"Yes," Nellie replied. "that's him."

"I remember him. I saw his photograph on the piano when the Colliers lived at Percy Circus."

Alice and Nellie arrived in mid-afternoon with plenty of time to spare. Jack wasn't due until after 3:30 p.m. but when they saw the number of soldiers milling about the platform, they were concerned they might not spot Jack, who would undoubtedly look much different than he had as a boy.

"Oh, my!" whispered Alice, "What shall we do, I wonder?"

Nellie stared at the crowd, and slowly shook her head from side to side.

"With them all dressed alike, and him so much older now, how will we know him?" asked Alice.

"Let's wait by the exit. We'll have a better chance of seeing him there as he comes out of the station."

A few minutes later, the doors of Jack's train opened, spilling khaki across the platform like a flash flood. Alice and Nellie stood on their toes in an effort to examine as many passing faces as they could.

"Oh, this is hopeless!" whined Nellie in desperation.

Jack elbowed his way through the crowd on the platform and performed a number of about-faces in the hope of seeing a teenage girl standing alone, *looking for someone*. No such girl was there as far as he could tell, and he wondered if he had been stood up. He remained on the platform, expecting Nellie to seek him out. All the while, she and Alice were just outside the exit. Minutes later, another train packed with servicemen arrived, and once more the platform filled to capacity with military uniforms.

Jack wished he had suggested another place to meet, but it was clearly too late for regrets. Convinced that Nellie had not come to meet him, he began making his way to the exit, but by then Nellie and Alice had given up. He exited the station with no particular destination in mind and walked aimlessly along Ferringdon Street, searching the passing faces for familiar features. All his old mates would be off to training camps or in France by now, so what was he to do on his own in London? He remembered the address Connie had given him for Nellie, but what if she had deliberately chosen *not* to meet him?

Jack put a match to the bowl of his pipe and looked through the smoke into the eyes of a young lady of about eighteen. She was looking directly at him and smiling. Something about her appeared vaguely familiar. Then, he saw Nellie hurrying toward the girl with the smile. In spite of the years that had passed, he was certain it was Nellie Marks.

"You don't know who I am, do you Jack?" the other girl asked.

Jack glanced quickly at Nellie, then back at the pretty stranger and stammered, "I'm sorry. Have we met?"

"You don't recognize me?" Alice teased, "Well, I'm not going to tell you. You'll just have to remember," she laughed.

Jack offered a couple of guesses, though he didn't really think either of them were very likely.

"It's Alice Geherty," laughed Nellie, "We went to Amwell Street School together, Remember?"

"Yes! Yes, I remember now, but you were just ten or eleven then. You mustn't fault me for not recognizing you. You've grown up."

"Thirteen," replied Alice with feigned indignation.

Alice, Nellie and Jack spent the rest of the day together, chatting excitedly about their favourite places in London, mutual friends and the war. The girls wanted to know everything about soldiering, and Jack enjoyed being the focus of their attention. They went to tea together at St. James's Park and walked to Trafalgar Square where a bent old man was feeding the pigeons amid the flutter of a hundred wings. Jack saw the girls home to Nellie's after a supper of fish and chips in Soho.

"Will we see you tomorrow?" queried Nellie.

Jack glanced at Alice and replied, "Yes, of course. We could spend the afternoon in Hyde Park or stroll along the embankment if you like."

The three said their goodbyes reluctantly, and Jack turned to leave, withdrawing a small booklet from his breast pocket as he walked. It had been given to him by the Canadian Y.M.C.A. supervisor at Shorncliffe and contained the address of the Queensborough Club.

"Sixty-seven Queensborough Terrace," muttered Jack to himself.

He returned the booklet to his pocket and took the underground to Bayswater Station, then walked the short distance to the Y.M.C.A. hostel near Hyde Park. The clubs promised Canadian troops safe, clean accommodation and provided a hot breakfast to boot.

The fresh sheets felt good when Jack climbed into his bunk, but sleep was slow to extinguish his thoughts. The last thing he remembered was the image of Alice's smile when their eyes met through tobacco smoke outside the station.

The following morning, the girls met Jack at Covent Garden. The three chatted and flirted as they strolled toward Piccadilly Circus to see the Shaftesbury Fountain. Alice withdrew a ha'penny from her hand bag, and with her eyes closed, tossed it into the water beneath Anteros. During lunch at *the Dog and Duck* on Soho's Bateman Street, Jack asked Alice and Nellie to write to him. Both of them promised they would.

"Alice has just obtained a position at the Army Pay Office on Regent Street," said Nellie, "She'll be starting in another week or so."

"Is that so?" replied Jack, turning to Alice with an exaggerated grin.

"I don't suppose you could slip a little extra into my pay packet then?" he joked.

Alice did subsequently begin work at the Army Pay Corps in July where she was paid twenty-three shillings weekly, almost four times the amount earned in her first job three years earlier.

Jack and Alice wrote to one another at every opportunity. Initially, they penned brief wishes for one another's well-being on postcards, signing them rather formally with their first and last names. In time, sealed envelopes replaced the postcards, the messages became lengthier and more personal, and the signatures shortened to 'Jack' and 'Alice.' Mail parades, always significant events for soldiers away from home, became especially important to Jack. When he received multiple pieces of mail, he often set Alice's letter aside until last, savouring it as he would a sweet dessert.

Jack spent every minute of his second leave with Alice, met her parents for the first time, and had Sunday dinner with them at their Cloudesley Road flat. Alice was excused from helping with the dishes, and the young couple sat together in the parlour talking about Canada, her holiday in Southborough the previous summer, and her favourite places in London. In early September, while sharing a bench in Berkley Square, Jack took her hand in his and nervously asked if he might have a lock of her hair to take with him when he went to France. When they parted Sunday evening, Jack kissed Alice goodbye.

Bombs continued to fall on England's cities throughout 1916. Residents were told to pull down their blinds and draw their curtains to prevent lights being seen by the airships' crews.

On the night of October 1st, Zeppelin L-31, commanded by Lieutenant Commander Heinrich Mathy, flew over London. Alice remembered that night in vivid detail. From her bedroom window at the back of the family flat on Cloudesley Road, she looked into a room on the top floor of a building on the next street. There was a man at a table with an acetylene lamp, in what was otherwise an empty room. It was all too suspicious, so she and her mum went to the police station to report what they had seen. They feared the man might be a German spy, signalling to the enemy zeppelins.

Zeppelin L-31

On their way home, Alice and her mum saw the ghostly shape of a zeppelin, caught in the sweep of a search-light above the city. They heard distant ground fire, but the pale grey airship continued on its way. Lieutenant Commander Mathy, Germany's foremost airship captain, jettisoned his bombs and began a long westward climb in an effort to rise above the clouds out of sight of his attackers. What Alice and her mother didn't see that night was a small, fragile bi-plane flown by Second Lieutenant 'Wolf' Tempest. The plane, hardly worthy of the name *fighter*, was equipped with a single light machine gun loaded with ammunition comprised of tracer and incendiary rounds. When Lieutenant Tempest fired into the airship, a luminescent glow appeared within the envelope of Mathy's zeppelin. A second later, the entire forward section of the hydrogen-filled giant erupted in a brilliant flash. Alice and her mum watched as the airship's white-hot aluminium skeleton glowed against the dark sky.

Mesmerized by the sight of the disintegrating monster, Alice shivered in the night air. As bits of burning debris fell from the distant wreckage, she heard a voice behind her attest, "That's 'er crew, that is."

Alice turned and saw a uniformed bobby gazing skyward.

Thirty-three-year-old Lieutenant Commander Mathy and his men plummeted to their deaths just north of the city. The gruesome image of fiery bits falling out of the night sky was burned into her memory, never to be erased.

On the stroke of midnight, the wreckage of Zeppelin L-31 crumpled onto a farmer's field at Potter's Bar. Mathy's body was discovered at dawn, embedded in the soft earth nearby. As soon as the airman's remains had been removed from the field, the farm's owner threw up a fence around the spot and began charging gawkers a shilling to see the imprint of the enemy's body in the soil.

CHAPTER TEN

DISTANT THUNDER

In mid-October, the Gehertys moved to 13 Coram Street, Holborn, and the 86th Canadian Machine Gun Battalion, which had been amalgamated with the Canadian Machine Gun School, was posted to Crowborough in Sussex. Jack and his mates were housed there in long wooden barracks, just wide enough for an aisle between two rows of twenty-four double bunks. He was quick to claim an upper bunk as he knew it would be warmer near the ceiling. Jack wrote to Alice, informing her of his change of address, and speculating how long it might be before the war separated them for months – *perhaps forever*.

Unable to arrange leave to go to London, Jack celebrated his 22nd birthday with his mates in the camp YMCA hut, a postcard bearing birthday wishes in his breast pocket. At the bottom of the delicately penned message were the words, "Love Alice."

In mid-December, Jack received a postcard from his brother, Frank, who was in the field somewhere in France. Now both of his brothers were on the continent, yet *there-he-was* still training in England. Sure, Joe had signed up months before him, but Frank hadn't enlisted until the 14th of September of 1915, a month after Jack. Frank didn't offer any details of the fight. He simply assured his brother that he was fine and wished him a "Merry Christmas."

Jack heard plenty of stories from those who had served in the line, most of whom had been wounded and were expecting to return to duty at the front. The war hadn't gone well for the allies in the first couple of years. The enemy had seized the high ground early on and fended off attacks with barbed wire and machine gun fire. Canadian forces, under British Command, were repeatedly assigned to suicidal charges against well defended positions with the same disastrous result time after time. Though the actual losses were withheld from the public at the time, the Second Battle of Ypres resulted in almost 6,000 Canadians killed or wounded in the spring of 1915. During the initial enemy assault on Canadian trenches, the German attackers employed poison gas for the very first time. Another 2,500 casualties were recorded at The Battle of Festubert in May, and in June of 1916, yet another 8,400 were lost at the Battle of Mont Sorrel, southeast of Ypres. Those waiting to be sent to the front heard only vague rumours about disturbingly high casualties among Canadian forces.

In late January, 1917, Jack read that the *Laurentic*, the ship that had taken him to Canada in 1910, struck a German mine and sank off the coast of Northern Ireland. He thought about the steward who had been especially kind to him throughout the voyage to Canada and wondered if the man had been aboard at the time of the sinking.

News of the Canadian Corps' successful assault on Vimy Ridge reached the Crowborough barracks on the 12th of April, even before the final objective was taken. Once again, reports of Canadian casualties were downplayed. Jack was proud to be part of the Canadian Expeditionary Force, but he felt he was missing out. He'd been in England almost eleven months, and the endless training was becoming unbearable. Later that morning, he was granted four days leave. He knew immediately what it meant and scribbled a post card to Alice to meet him at Waterloo Station.

Neither of them worried about finding one another this time. Alice even knew which carriage Jack was most likely to occupy. She spotted him almost as soon as he stepped onto the platform.

"Four days!" squealed Alice when Jack told her the news.

Then she saw the look in Jack's eyes and realized something had been left unsaid.

Alice's familiar smile vanished in an instant, "Oh, Heavens! You're going to France!"

Every muscle in her body stiffened as she waited for Jack to confirm her worst fear.

"Let's find a place to talk," Jack said curtly.

As soon as the Gehertys heard the news, they invited Jack to stay with them. Alice beamed when her father refused to let Jack spend his last leave in a hostel with strangers. The young man protested half-heartedly, but Peter assured him they could fit a borrowed cot into the parlour, or if necessary, Jack could have twelve-year-old Arthur's bed.

"Arthur can sleep on the sofa," offered Rosina, "He'll think it a great adventure, I'm sure."

The day before Jack returned to camp, Alice asked him to accompany her to a photographer's studio, so she would have a picture by which to remember him while he was away in France.

Jack consented and they set out to a shop on Victoria Street near the station. Above the shop entrance hung a modest black and gold sign which read, 'Wykeham Studios Ltd.' They went to *The Albert*, a nearby pub, for lunch while the photographer processed the film and made a print. By the time they got back to Coram Street, Alice had removed the portrait from its protective envelope three times to admire it. She cherished that photo of Jack for the rest of her life.

Jack returned to Crowborough on the evening of the 17th of April. The following morning, he was posted to the Canadian Machine Gun Depot Pool, and told to get his kit in order for embarkation to France.

Jack landed at La Havre at the mouth of the River Seine at first light on April 19, 1917. A steady rain had fallen through the night and persisted throughout the day. Once in France, Jack was kept on the move in a northerly direction until he reached the French port of Etaples late the following afternoon.

Private John Albert "Jack" Collier, 5th Machine Gun Company

Etaples was a major allied distribution centre on a functioning rail line that ended at the nearby village of Camiers. The railway connected to the towns and villages west of the front line, and for that reason, it was an ideal location for receiving and treating the wounded. As a result, there were four field hospitals in the village, and by the end of the Great War, more than 10,000 young men lie buried in the nearby Etaples Military Cemetery.

Jack made his way to the Canadian Corps' Machine Gun Pool at Camiers. The pool consisted of thoroughly trained, albeit mostly inexperienced, machine gunners held in reserve for field units in need of replacements. A cluster of damp and draughty tents provided temporary accommodation for those who stood in the wings, awaiting their debut performance in The Great War. They slept on thin mattresses atop iron cots. A few feet away, the tents and huts of No. 22 General Hospital were capable of sheltering up to 2,370 wounded combatants while they awaited evacuation to England, or in some cases, their hurried return to the line.

The Battle of Arras, which had begun on the ninth of April, was behaving like a magnet, drawing fresh troops out of England, across the Channel, and into the trenches of northern France. The offensive was about to provide Jack with his first taste of direct enemy fire. After all the marching, the polishing of boots and brass, and the endless hours of training, Jack's courage was about to be tested. He was concerned about how he might react. How would he perform when the time came? To Jack, lying on a rusting cot in the dark, the exploding shells at the front sounded like distant thunder. In just days, he would experience the ear-splitting cacophony of artillery barrages and inhale the acrid odour of cordite.

The front meandered 400 miles between the North Sea and the border of Switzerland, and Jack had no idea where, along that wandering line, he might be sent. The army, mysterious and all-powerful, was not about to tell him until it was damned-good-and-ready. Day after day, he awaited his orders while the anxiety grew in the pit of his stomach.

Finally, on the 27th, Private John A. Collier No. 174535 was struck off the strength of the Machine Gun Pool and posted to the 5th Machine Gun Company. The unit, comprised entirely of machine gun crews, was called "The Fifth" because it was attached to the 5th Infantry Brigade of the Canadian Expeditionary Force's 2nd Division. The reassignment was Jack's *moment of destiny*, because within four months, it would put him in exactly the wrong place at precisely the wrong time.

Lieutenants Grantham and Creighton of the 5th Machine Gun Company were in Camiers to witness a demonstration of 'indirect fire.' The replacements assigned to the machine gun company, including Jack, accompanied the two officers on their return to the unit's field headquarters. They boarded the train on the 28th and proceeded at a snail's pace amid military bureaucracy and delays due to enemy action. No passenger carriage this time – Jack and his comrades sat with their backs against the interior wall of a box-car.

While the little group of Canadians enjoyed the relative comfort of a dry rail-car, the war diary of the 5th Machine Gun Company reported 162,000 rounds of small arms ammunition expended within two and a half hours amid a light drizzle. The daily account of the company's activities also reported three 'Other Ranks' killed, and three wounded.

The following day, Jack joined his unit on the east side of Vimy Ridge, along a railway embankment between the villages of Vimy and Farbus. There, toward the southern end of the recently taken ridge, the weather was windy and unseasonably cold, and the sky was over-stuffed with various shades of grey cloud. A two-day battle for the village of Arleux-en-Gohelle was drawing to a close though heavy shelling continued. Ten days had elapsed since he had stepped onto French soil; ten days without once firing a shot in the enemy's direction. It had been a period of acclimatization and acceptance of his new reality. With his senses overwhelmed by continual exposure to new experiences, Jack's home and family were almost forgotten. He was, in those first days, entirely focused on the present.

The Allied advance known as the Battle of Arras had ground to a halt though officially it continued into mid-May. Combatants on both sides hunkered down in rat-infested trenches and hurled artillery shells at one another in an attempt to kill and maim as many as possible. Brilliant flashes of light turned the nights inside out. Exploding shells generated ripples in the puddles that reflected their glare. Eyes and ears were left numb and useless for several long seconds after each blast. Sleep proved tenuous, fragmented and thin.

On May 1, a shell landed in the trench around dawn. Before Jack had the opportunity to know either of them, the lifeless bodies of Private Bill Apt and Sergeant Hipkins were being carried to the rear on stretchers. The following day another member of the company's twenty-two crews was wounded, and the night after that, another gun crew was hit. Private Graham, the Number One, was killed while two others were wounded – one so severely that he died a few hours later.

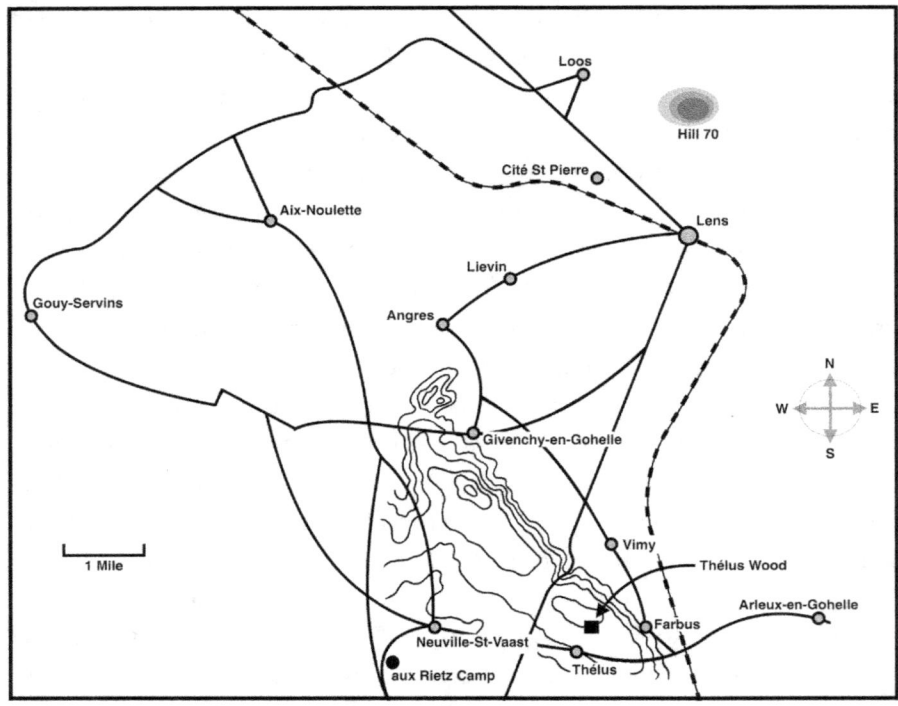

Map showing area of the battle.

Life among the battle-torn trenches and craters was barely tolerable. Months of artillery bombardment had disrupted the area's natural drainage, leaving countless water-filled craters contaminated with the blood and flesh of horses and men. Jack's great-coat was thoroughly caked with French mud by his third day in the line.

During the early morning hours of May 8, the 5th Machine Gun Company's scheduled relief was temporarily disrupted by an enemy assault on their position. Withdrawn to the aux Rietz rest camp, a half-mile southwest of Neuville-St-Vaast, the machine gun crews found themselves bathing by evening. Though Jack had only been in the line nine days, to him it seemed much longer. Those first few days of combat were disorienting and peppered with surges of adrenalin, but he was becoming familiar with the tangle of trenches and craters as well as the men on whom his life depended. Though shells had thrown up filth and hot shrapnel within a few feet of his crew, they had made it through those nine days without injury. Decades later, as an aging veteran, Jack admitted to feeling, "a little uneasy."

For the first time since boarding the train in Camiers, Jack found the time to write a quick note to Alice, but he did not share his recently acquired perception of war.

Canadian Machine Gun Crews in April 1917

On May 9, the men of The Fifth began the day with PT followed by a quartermaster parade; then they cleaned their weapons. A pay parade was held on the 10th after PT, and at 4 p.m. on the 11th, the company was ordered back into the line on Vimy Ridge. Jack's section was assigned to the western edge of Thélus Wood. The weather was bitterly cold and just after dawn on the 12th of May, wet wind-driven snow fell for an hour.

The company was relieved on May 20th for a week's rest. Relief occurred, as usual, under cover of darkness to minimize casualties. Still, one man died before he could reach the relative safety of the rest area at aux Rietz Camp. The machine gun crews spent their rest-days on anti-aircraft duty, attending shortage parades, overhauling equipment, inspections and sessions of elementary drill. When it wasn't raining, the company's four sections formed teams and played competitive baseball.

Jack found the time to write postcards to his mum, his brothers, and Alice. He knew how important it was for those at home to know that he was okay. He had felt the burden of worry while at Shorncliffe and Crowborough when his brothers neglected to write for a while.

Weeks earlier, Jack had explained to Alice that his correspondence from the front would be censored, and that he would not be able to tell her where he was. Still, each time she received a postcard from him, she was both delighted to find him safe and disappointed with the lack of detail in his messages.

My Dear Alice,   *May 22, 1917*

I have just now received your letter of the 16th and I am glad to hear you are well. We are out and resting a week – even had a bath! Its cold today, plenty of food but not as good as your Mum's.

Do take care of yourself.

Love Jack

Alice always read Jack's postcards several times before putting them into a Peak, Frean & Company biscuit tin which she kept under her bed. Some nights, when she slipped beneath the covers, she would reach under the bed for the tin, open it, and read them again before turning out the lamp and going to sleep.

The 5th Machine Gun Company was back in the line by the evening of the 27th of May.

Jack spent hours crouched in sticky mud behind his Vickers Mark I machine gun. Somewhere, just over his left shoulder, 3,600 young men had traded their lives for victory the previous month. Another 7,000 had been wounded as the Canadians rushed up the western slope of Vimy Ridge behind a creeping barrage. Had they not taken their objectives on April 9 and fought off counterattacks over the next three days, Jack would not have been able to occupy his position overlooking the ridge's eastern slope.

Lieutenant Grantham announced that the entire 2nd Division was to be taken out of the line for a month's rest. Jack couldn't believe his luck. He had only just arrived a month ago, whereas some of his comrades had been at the front for months with only brief respites out of the line.

Shortly after midnight on the 3rd of June, the company was relieved and marched to aux Rietz Camp for a rest and breakfast. With appetites satiated, Jack's battle-weary gun crew were transported to billets at Chateau Dou la Hay in Gouy-Servins, where they could enjoy the comfort of a roof over their heads, ten miles from the front. Much of the window glazing was gone, as was the furniture, but one could stay relatively dry by sleeping in a corner beyond the reach of the wind and rain.

CHAPTER ELEVEN

FRENCH MUD AND MUSTARD GAS

Over the next twenty-eight days, the men of the 5th Machine Gun Company bathed, slept, trained and drilled. Their training included map reading, firing range practice, and the testing of box respirators, the Canadians' most recently introduced defence against gas.

Initially, Canadian soldiers were told to soak any available piece of cloth in water or their own urine if necessary, and cover their nose and mouth with it to filter out the noxious fumes. Then, combatants were issued crude, semi-effective hood-masks made of chemically impregnated canvas with viewing windows of vision-distorting mica. They were unpopular for several reasons, one of which was that the mica clouded over almost as soon as the hood was put on, severely impairing the wearer's vision. In addition, the chemicals in the canvas burned one's forehead as well as the neck, where the hood was tucked into the collar. Rumours that soldiers had been asphyxiated by a build-up of carbon dioxide inside the hood circulated through the trenches. No one wanted to put the equipment on, and when driven to do so by fear, they took it off at the first indication that the gas had passed or dissipated.

Small Box Respirators, or SBRs as they were known, had many weaknesses too. They were delicate, ill-fitting, hot and prone to failure while providing inadequate protection at best. Because the face-masks incorporated a snorkel-like mouth piece and nose pincers, soldiers were unable to communicate, and breathing through the one-inch corrugated tube with a box of charcoal at its end required powerful lungs. Soldiers routinely removed them when condensation on the lenses prevented them from seeing what they were doing, and many suffered the consequences. The SBR's most alarming shortcoming was that it wasn't designed to prevent the excruciating burns caused by sulphur mustard, a gas which hadn't yet made its appearance on the battlefield. That would not happen until July 12, while the 5th Machine Gun Company was out of the line, but at the time, SBRs were all the army had to offer.

World War One Small Box Respirator training.

Throughout their rest at Gouy-Servins, the company paraded for equipment inspections, early morning PT, and Sunday religious services. With somewhat more enthusiasm, they mustered to collect their pay and precious mail from home.

Jack received a number of letters and postcards, two of which were from Alice, but neither of them contained much detail about her life in London. Instead, they focused on questions about his well-being. At the end of each, she implored him to write as soon as he could find the time. Jack retrieved a short pencil from his tunic pocket and began writing, but he wasn't about to share what he had experienced at the front. His replies said nothing of the fear, the shells, or the lifeless bodies on stretchers. Instead, he wrote about the camp, its amenities and its shortcomings, all the while assuring her that he was well and safe.

Lieutenant Grantham organized sports competitions, pitting the company's four sections against one another. He even authorized a wet canteen on one occasion, but Jack, who never found beer very appealing, showed little interest in the otherwise celebrated event. While the company was out of the line, a few men, entitled by lengthy service at the front, were granted ten-day leaves to Britain, Paris and lesser destinations in France. Jack, who had been with the unit for only five weeks, would not be eligible for a very long time.

A favourite pastime at the front was playing cards, and Jack's preferred game was cribbage. Wooden matches served as pegs, but a cribbage board proved a clumsy bit of kit, so being a glove-cutter by trade, Private Collier solved the problem with a thick piece of leather horse harness. Using a pencil, he laid out precisely aligned rows of holes on the two-inch-wide strap and borrowed a leather punch from the quartermaster. With the skill and precision of his trade, he fashioned a serviceable cribbage board which, when folded in half, fit into his tunic pocket.

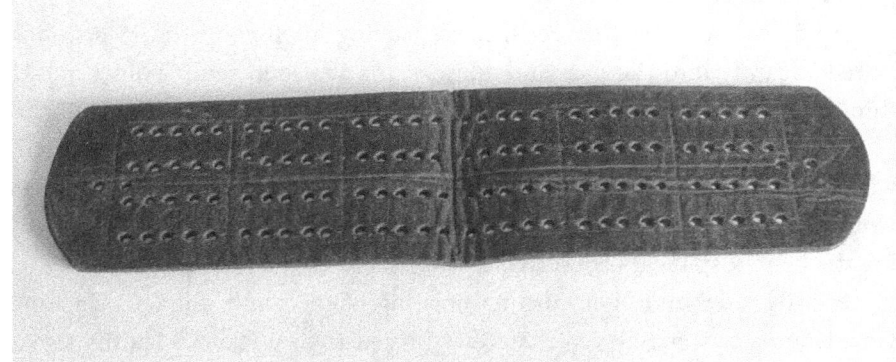

Private John A. Collier's handcrafted leather cribbage board.

The company's rest ended at 10:30 a.m. on the 1st of July when the troops moved off to billets in Aix-Noulette. There, they slept in full kit within 5,500 yards of the front line, well within the effective range of enemy field guns. In the late evening of the 2nd of July, they re-entered the line near Lens, but C-Section failed to complete the relief operation until 6 a.m. on the 3rd due to an estimated 8,000 rounds of incoming artillery. Sergeant Shorts and one "other rank" were killed, and four men, including Lieutenant Taylor, were wounded.

Jack and his gun crew advanced toward their assigned position along a railway trench until the train they were riding was blocked by fallen trees. He and his mates dismounted and continued on foot. Jack, bent beneath the weight of the tripod on his shoulders, led the way. The others carried the gun and wooden boxes of ammunition while shells exploded around them. The men danced their way forward, wincing and ducking as they went. Out of nowhere, a shell struck the trench just ahead of Jack, and in an instant, his world went dark.

"Collier's down!" came a shout from behind.

Jack's crew hurried to his aid, freed him from the sticky mud, and helped him to his feet. The soft earth had absorbed the shock, so the shell had failed to detonate, but its impact had knocked Jack to his knees and almost buried him in viscous mud. The men put on a brave face, cracked a couple of macabre jokes, and continued on their way.

The following day, Jack heard that the seriously wounded Lieutenant Taylor had died before reaching the casualty clearing station. It was a sobering bit of bad news.

As he sat in his leather recliner re-packing his pipe in the 1980s, Jack stared vacantly into the past and, almost in a whisper, said, "Sometimes, I think I was lucky to come back alive."

Heavy shelling continued throughout the first week of July. Private Pettit, with whom Jack had played cribbage during their month out of the line, was wounded on the seventh, and like Lieutenant Taylor, died without ever seeing the field hospital at Camiers.

Shortly after midnight, on the morning of the tenth, the 5th Machine Gun Company was relieved. Its crews lugged their Vickers Maxims seven miles to billets in Aix-Noulette to rest. The ground still shook there, and the rattle of distant gunfire disrupted their sleep, but the food was hot and their beds were dry, so the term "rest" wasn't entirely inappropriate. They spent the next day servicing their weapons and preparing to march two miles further west to Bouvigny Huts the following morning.

At Bouvigny Huts, still within reach of the Kaiser's long-range guns, a building was hit during the night, and forty-two soldiers belonging to another unit were killed. Jack was detailed to help retrieve the corpses, lift them onto stretchers, and arrange them side by side to await a burial detail. They all wore the same khaki wool battledress as Jack and appeared to be about his age. Their vacant eyes and boyish faces shook Jack's courage. It was a disturbing sight; a macabre memory that could never be erased.

On the twelfth, the company paraded first for PT at 6:30 a.m. then again at 9:00 a.m. to bath. In the afternoon they were issued replacements for damaged and lost articles of clothing and equipment.

The men of The Fifth were unaware that late that evening, the Jerries deployed mustard gas for the first time, firing shells marked with yellow crosses into allied lines. Neither the victims nor their officers knew anything about the new gas which, unlike previous chemical weapons, polluted trenches and shell-holes and permeated clothing. Invisible, it remained potent for days after being deployed. In many cases, casualties didn't know they were being gassed until it was too late; until their eyes and exposed skin began to burn. Coughing, blinded, and suffering excruciating pain, mustard gas victims could do nothing to stop the progression of their symptoms and had to be evacuated to hospital.

Jack and his No. Two, Harry Johnson, slept like hibernating bears that night. When the company formed up for PT at 6:30 a.m. he and his pal were nowhere to be seen. Lieutenant Robinson was livid.

"Where the Hell is Johnson, and where's that bloody Collier?" he screamed to no one in particular.

The lieutenant sent a corporal to find the missing men while he lectured the rest of the parade about the potential penalties for slacking off. Later in the day, the pair were paraded before Captain McCorkle who formally charged the two miscreants with the offence. A week later, Jack's sentence was recorded on his official military record. Still today, Library and Archives Canada hold a digital image of Jack's form MFW 54 containing a single line relating to his crime. It reads, "19.7.17 Forfeits 2 days Pay for when on Active Service absent from 6:30 a.m. Parade." The 5th Machine Gun Company was back in the Lens sector trenches by then.

At about half-ten on the 21st of July, a lieutenant observed an enemy bi-plane monitoring the British trenches from afar. He lowered his binoculars, turned toward Jack, and ordered him to fire at the winged observer. Jack, who had undergone extensive machine gun training for more than a year before arriving in France, was confident that he knew more about his weapon than did the junior officer.

"Sir," protested Jack, "it's two miles away, and the Vickers's effective range is less than twenty-two-hundred yards."

"That was an order, Private," shouted the subaltern.

"But Sir," Jack argued, "we'll give away our position!"

"God-dammit, man, I'll have you court-marshalled!" screamed the officer.

Sensing the confrontation was beginning to erode his veneer of authority, the officer turned to Private Thibodeau on his left.

"Soldier," he spewed, "fire on that plane!"

"I'd never hit it from here, Sir," objected Thibodeau wryly, whereupon the lieutenant strode toward him, commandeered the gun, and fired the Mark I Maxim in the general direction of the plane, expending two full belts of ammunition in quick succession. The gun was well on its way to overheating when the firing finally came to an end. Collier and Thibodeau exchanged looks as the distant plane droned along the horizon unaffected. The officer, red-faced with anger, stomped off along the trench.

"Bloody fool," growled Thibodeau.

About four hours later, just after 2 p.m. Jack's position was heavily shelled for thirty minutes. Three men were killed, including an officer who was passing through the line, his runner, and one of the machine gun company's own. Jack, seething with anger, helped carry one of the bodies to the nearest communication trench.

On the 28th of July, thirty-two men, led by Lieutenant Malcolm, were assigned by Captain McCorkle to transport boxes of .303 ammunition to a forward position. The desperately needed cargo was secured to racks attached to the harnesses of sixteen mules. Jack, himself a mere 125 pounds, hefted the 80-pound boxes along with his mates, Johnson, Thoms, Cohen and Cornwall, and at 10 p.m. they set off toward a recently captured German trench two miles away.

As they neared their destination, the enemy began shelling the area. White-hot flashes lit the war-torn terrain like strobe lights, casting long shadows that danced and veered erratically over the broken ground. The explosions momentarily deafened those in the vicinity. When the detail finally arrived at its destination, Lieutenant Malcolm ordered the men to unload the ammunition on the double and ride the mules back to their starting point. Jack, clinging to a mule's harness on his return to the rear, passed in front of an allied field gun just as a shell left its barrel. By an unlucky coincidence, the faulty shell exploded prematurely. The resulting concussion slammed Jack's helmet down over his face. Deafened, temporarily blinded by the flash, dazed and bleeding from his nose, he clung to the metal hooks to which the ammo boxes had recently been attached.

When he opened his eyes, two blurred silhouettes loomed before him in the glare of the battle. With adrenalin pumping through veins, Jack took them to be Huns who had jumped down into the trench in front of him. For a second, he thought he was about to die, but as his numbed senses returned, he realized the silhouettes were the ears of the mule he was riding.

Finally, at 6 a.m. having covered less than four miles in eight hours amid the confusion of the bombardment, the men arrived back at their starting point. With his right hand bandaged where a piece of the shell's shrapnel had struck him, and dried blood on his upper lip and chin, Jack recounted his tale of a couple of enemy soldiers that turned out to be mule ears. The men of The Fifth roared with laughter.

During July, the war ended for seventeen men of the 5th Machine Gun Company, six of whom were buried in France. The other eleven were wounded severely enough to warrant evacuation to England where the sheets were clean and the tea was hot. Still, few envied them for more than a fleeting second. They each suffered excruciating pain, and some were likely to have lost a limb or an eye.

The army, locked into rigid procedures and protocols, routinely recorded the number of bullets used each day. It was an indication of the intensity of conflict. The 5th Machine Gun Company's report for July indicated 177,250 rounds of small arms ammunition expended.

The British launched an offensive in Flanders on July 31, in part, to deprive the enemy of access to continental ports along the east end of the English Channel. It was the beginning of the Third Battle of Ypres, also known as Passchendaele. The British High Command proposed a diversionary attack in the south to draw German resources away from the coast, so Lieutenant-General Currie's Canadian Corps was tasked with taking the city of Lens. Currie, however, recognized the strategic importance of Hill 70, a mere 2,000 yards north of the city. Though briefly held by the British in 1915, it had since been in enemy hands. By the summer of 1917, it was riddled with German trenches, tunnels and underground bunkers and defended by machine guns in concrete pill-boxes. Wrapped in thousands of coils of razor wire, Hill 70 overlooked Len's northern perimeter and had to be taken before any assault on the city could hope to succeed.

At midnight on August 1, Jack's unit was deployed to the forward trenches at Cité St. Pierre, a village located a mile or so west of the German-held city of Lens. Hill 70 was just a few hundred yards away. The Enemy's artillery was unusually active throughout the first week, but the Canadian trenches and gun positions were well fortified, and Sergeant Morson was the only one reported wounded.

It was impossible for the men in the trenches to see the big picture. They relied solely on rumours and what they witnessed with their own eyes. They simply did as they were ordered and either trusted, or in some cases, despised their officers. The "brass hats," as they were known, seldom shared much of what they knew, yet there was a feeling among the men of the 5th that something was up – something big!

For two weeks the front remained more or less stationary while the details of the Canadian assault on Hill 70 were refined and rehearsed. Jack Collier was one of 7,000 Canadians that formed a line stretching from Lens to Bois Hugo, two miles to the north. On the evening of the 14th of August, the Canadians began a bombardment of the hill that continued throughout the night. Eight gun crews of the 5th Machine Gun Company cleaned their weapons in preparation for going over the parapet in the morning.

The build-up of men and materiel hadn't gone unnoticed by the enemy, and in anticipation of an attack, they targeted the Canadian trenches with gas during the night. At 4:25 a.m. ten battalions of the 1st and 2nd Canadian Divisions emerged from their trenches and charged the German defenders behind a rolling artillery barrage. The 2nd Division, with the 5th Brigade on its left flank, was in the centre with the 1st on its left and the 4th on its right. The 3rd Division stood down in reserve. The attack advanced up a gentle grade through Bois Rasé, a shattered woodland, in low light. German trenches on Hill 70 were simultaneously targeted by more than 200 eighteen-pounders, and a creeping barrage advanced just ahead of the infantry as they stumbled over the shell-torn landscape. Accompanied by kilted pipers, the assault continued through broken wire to the enemy trenches at the base of the hill. The handful of German soldiers, who remained with their dead and wounded, surrendered almost immediately.

The 1st Division captured Hill 70 while the 2nd secured Cité St Edouard and Cité St Laurent. Having accomplished their first objective in twenty minutes, the Canadians paused to reorganize. Support units brought up additional ammunition and stretchers while enemy artillery shells screamed into the stationary battalions, killing and maiming indiscriminately. After twenty minutes, the attackers pushed on, taking Cité St Elisabeth and Cité St Emile, but failing in their final objective, the seizure of the chalk quarry north of Cité St Auguste.

Hill 70 was firmly in the hands of the Canadian Corps, but the worst fighting was yet to come. Fifteen German battalions launched counter-attacks throughout the afternoon and evening. Still, the Canadian line held, and soon after dark, hostilities waned as the combatants on both sides rested. More than 1,000 young Canadians lay dead in the French mud, and 2,500 awaited evacuation for treatment of their wounds.

The 5th Canadian Machine Gun Company suffered ten casualties, three of whom were killed when D Section's No. 3 Gun took a direct hit from an artillery shell. Harry O'Brien, Al Tremblay and Everett Marryatt were all men with whom Jack had trained, eaten and slept. Perhaps the reason he kept a framed picture of the Vimy Memorial on his bedroom wall until his own death was, in part, because those names are engraved on the monument.

On the 16th, Canadian forces wrestled the chalk quarry away from the enemy who, through the night, launched sulphur-mustard shells into the Canadian line. The creeping mustard gas vapours blistered skin, seared lungs and indiscriminately blinded any who were exposed to its fumes.

German counterattacks on the 17th and 18th were repelled though not without massive casualties. Low-flying enemy aircraft fired into the Canadian trenches until four guns of C Section were assigned to anti-aircraft duty. The defenders faced another new and terrifying weapon for the first time when the German Army employed crude flamethrowers against their front line. Still, they clung tenaciously to the captured hill and the surrounding villages. The Vickers Maxims of the 5th Machine Gun Company sprayed 50,000 rounds of ammunition eastward every twenty-four hours.

The 2nd Division launched a series of attacks on Lens over the next couple of days. Jack and his machine gun crew provided supporting fire during those assaults and thus became preferred targets. During one attack, a shell exploded nearby, exhuming the carcass of a partially decomposed horse, a casualty of a previous action. The diminutive glove-cutter from Hamilton, now a warrior in a struggle for survival, was then within hours of a life-changing encounter with fate.

CHAPTER TWELVE

A WOMAN'S VOICE

The Hague Declaration of 1899 prohibited the use of gas as a weapon of war. Nevertheless, the Imperial German Army began employing phosgene and chlorine gas near Ypres, Belgium, less than a year into the Great War. Thereafter, both they and, to a lesser degree, the British used gas to terrorize one another. It was particularly effective in World War One because it was the first time in history that troops were more or less stationary, sheltering in trenches from relentless artillery bombardments. The newly developed Mustard gas, not deployed by the Germans until the summer of 1917, was delivered by what came to be known as Yellow-Cross shells, so named because they were marked with a painted yellow cross. The heavier-than-air sulphur mustard vapours crept along the ground, seeking the lowest terrain like an invisible liquid. On a still night, the pernicious gas might remain at the bottom of a trench or a shell crater for hours. It accounted for 21,000 casualties between August 1917 and November 1918. 4,000 of its victims died.

When the gas gongs sounded, men up and down the line donned their respirators, as they had been trained – *and then they prayed*. Often, the gas slithered into a trench like a malevolent apparition without being detected. Such was the case "just left of Loos – in front of Lens" shortly after 4:35 a.m. on August 21, 1917. Two khaki-clad figures hunkered against the trembling wall of the recently captured *Old German Line 2*, enduring the ground-shaking concussions of explosive shells fired by the German 6th Army. "Five-Nines" struck the sodden mud just yards from the trench, raining loathsome filth and hot shrapnel onto its cowering occupants.

When the bombardment paused, the machine gunner and his number two momentarily relaxed their tightened muscles. A crescent moon glowed indistinctly through a gauze-like cloud cover. With his ears still ringing, Jack searched the shadowy terrain for movement among the shadows. He listened for sounds coming from the featureless depths of no-man's-land. Distant thunder-like booms testified to the persistence of foe and ally alike.

By the time Jack and his comrades smelled the horseradish-like odour and felt the initial effects of the sulphur mustard, the damage had been done. Their exposed skin, and especially their eyes, had begun to burn. His reflexes dulled by fatigue, Jack gasped, "GAS!" and groped clumsily for his respirator in the canvas pouch on his chest. Fear and desperation gripped the young soldier as he fumbled in the gloom. The burning sensation in his throat told him he had already sucked fumes into his lungs.

Someone nearby yelled, "GAS!" and banged frantically on a brass shell casing with a bayonet.

> Gas! GAS! Quick, boys! – An ecstasy of fumbling,
> Fitting the clumsy helmets just in time;
> But someone still was yelling out and stumbling
> And flound'ring like a man in fire or lime...
> Dim, through the misty panes and thick green light,
> As under a green sea, I saw him drowning.
> – Wilfred Owen

With his protective mask finally in place, Jack gulped for air and blinked continuously in an effort to flush his burning eyes with tears. He wanted to spit the awful taste from his mouth, but had been trained to not remove his mask for even an instant. Within a few seconds, his lips, tongue and nostrils were ablaze with searing pain. Large blisters began forming on the exposed skin of his hands, wrists, neck and face. Mercilessly, they invaded his mouth, nostrils and lungs, awakening millions of nerve endings. He struggled for air, never able to suck in quite what his lungs demanded. Though every breath had become indescribably painful, the reflex to take in oxygen was irresistible. Jack was in agony and quickly lost his ability to function. He writhed helplessly in a confused semi-conscious state amid the gas at the bottom of the trench. Someone took hold of his tunic and dragged him roughly along the wooden duckboards, around a corner, and into a communication trench.

At the moment of Jack's agony, Alice was asleep in her bed at 13 Coram Street, a ticking alarm clock beside her head on the night table. It would awaken her two hours and twenty-five minutes later, and she would routinely begin another day, unaware of Jack's fate. Though always anxious about his well-being, she would assume that he was alright when she climbed into bed that warm August night.

> *War Diary of the 5th Canadian Machine Gun Company*
> *2nd Canadian Division*
> 21.8.17 Enemy shelled Trench at N.8.a.6.7. to N.8.a.7.5. very heavily. This shelling reached a climax at 4.35 a.m. Zero Hour when the brigade on our right made an advance. The Enemy held his Barrage down for one hour. The Barrage Guns of this Unit assisted by using Barrage Fire expending 19,500 Rds. S.A.A. – Casualties (WOUNDED 3 O.R.'s) Gassed

Jack, now a nameless statistic, joined the hundreds of thousands of anonymous "other ranks" on both sides who'd soon be forgotten by those still fighting for survival. The war diary of the 5th Canadian Machine Gun Company recorded his nightmare in the final line of the day's entry. His story was told in the detached language of military bureaucracy.

Combat afforded little time for sympathy, nor was there more than a fleeting moment amid the horrors of the battlefield for remembering. Men came and went. Most, outside of a handful of Jack's closest comrades, were too preoccupied with their own survival to notice that he was no longer among them. While being swept along by the 2nd Division's eastward advance, a select few wondered if he had lived or died.

Jack didn't remember much after those first horrific moments. The rest of the night was a foggy blur of choking, chest and abdominal pain, vomiting, coughing up mucus, disorientation and apprehension. He couldn't die yet. He and Alice had plans. He had promised her that, *when the war ended...* his rational thoughts sank into a sea of delirium.

Jack's vague recollections included being bounced along on a stretcher as his bearers stumbled and lurched through trenches and over uneven ground. He couldn't catch his breath and felt like he was suffocating. The intense pain in his eyes overwhelmed his attempts to open them. He simply couldn't manage it, nor could he speak with what felt like a mouthful of burning coals. Voices were muffled and blurred beyond recognition. At the dressing station,

The severely wounded lay on stretchers awaiting transport to a dressing station.

someone poured a little water onto his lips and applied bandages to his hands and face. His anonymous caregiver spoke to him, but he couldn't understand what they were saying.

"I can't breathe," he whispered so faintly that no one heard. Such were his memories. Then he was left lying on a litter on the ground for what seemed to him an eternity.

Swimming in a sea of confusion and barely conscious, Jack was lifted into a motor ambulance. He was one of forty-two men that the No. 8 Canadian Field Ambulance rushed to the main dressing station at Noeux-Les-Mines that day. The men of The Number Eight did that every day, week after week; month after month, throughout the war.

Jack had no memory of the ten-mile ride. Perhaps he lapsed into unconsciousness, but he remembered being unloaded and carried a short distance. Then he felt his feet and legs rise higher than his head, and realized he was being carried down stairs. He counted the jolts as his rescuers descended into a subterranean abyss and calculated he was three levels below ground.

Jack thought he heard a muffled voice inquire, "What's your name?"

"John," he answered in a whisper.

More garbled sounds resembling questions followed, but Jack was too exhausted to reply, even if he had understood what had been asked. Anonymous hands cut away every item of his clothing. Then, a solution of sodium bicarbonate was applied liberally to his skin. At the same time, a set of unseen fingers forced his eyelids apart and washed his unseeing eyes. The treatment wasn't dramatically effective, but it was the only option available in 1917, and it seemed to ease the pain a little. Next, his head and neck were wrapped in gauze, so only his nostrils and mouth were exposed. His blistered, bleeding hands were cleaned and dressed in an effort to prevent infection, as were parts of his thighs and groin where perspiration had intensified the effects of the gas. Pain was to be Jack's companion for the foreseeable future.

Sulphur mustard vapours attack the bronchial tubes, stripping off the mucous membrane and causing internal bleeding. It took some fatally injured soldiers four or five weeks to die.

Jack had no concept of time. He could neither see nor speak, and his hearing was significantly impaired. He worried that he had been permanently blinded; even wondered if he would live. Anxiety gripped him mercilessly as he contemplated a life devoid of images. He could still see Alice's gentle face in his mind, but worried that eventually, he'd lose even that. When he tried to inquire about his condition, his voice sounded strangely distant and unintelligible. He could make out no discernible response among the blurred symphony of urgent voices around him. Jack slipped mercifully into unconsciousness.

Over the next few hours, the young private drifted in and out of awareness, unsure where he was or what was happening around him. In fact, his evacuation was continuing thirty miles northwest to the 58th Casualty Clearing Station west of Longuenesse where he would await transport to a field hospital by train.

Jack awakened periodically, coughing and gasping for air. He felt continuous jostling and bumping. Was he being carried or riding in a vehicle of some sort – a train perhaps? He couldn't be sure, and he didn't much care. He wanted to escape through sleep from the sensation of being on fire, and from his apprehension about his future.

Late on Thursday, August 23, Jack arrived at 22 General Hospital in Camiers where he became one of 347 casualties admitted that day. By day's end, the hospital's tents held 1,163 patients. With his vision still severely impaired and his mind numbed by the trauma of the past couple of days, he was barely aware of his surroundings. Still, he thought he felt raindrops on his face as his stretcher was carried into what he sensed was some sort of structure. When he was lifted onto a cot inside, he heard bed-springs squeak. Then someone spoke rather loudly. He heard the word, "hospital" clearly.

Without opening his eyes, Jack croaked, "Where? Where am I?"

"You're in a little French town called Camiers" responded a second voice.

Jack was surprised, first because he managed to make out every word, and second because the voice was that of a woman. She had a distinctly English accent, and her scent was warm and wonderful. It reminded him of his last day in London, the memory of which the trenches had almost stolen from him.

Having spent a week at the Machine Gun Pool at Camiers four months earlier, Jack was familiar with the white hospital tents just a couple of hundred yards away from his quarters, but he hadn't given them a great deal of thought at the time. Perhaps he didn't want to think about them then, just days before going to the front.

"Who are you?" Jack inquired hoarsely.

"I'm Miss Henderson, your nurse."

Jack tried to smile beneath the layered wraps of gauze on his face. Gentle hands tucked the bedding snugly around his body. Then, he heard Miss Henderson's footsteps recede across the wooden floor, and felt an inexplicable wave of emotion wash over him. He hadn't heard a female voice for months, and for the first time in what seemed like an eternity, he felt safe and warm.

Jack's chest felt bruised from the endless coughing. It began to heave in yet another fit of breath-robbing coughs as he lay on his cot in the evening gloom. After a minute or two of gasping for air, he asked no one in particular, "What time is it?"

When no one replied, Jack realized the nurses were likely busy with duties elsewhere, and the nearby patients, if there were any, were either asleep or not up to talking. He listened to the rattle of rain on the tent's canvas and the shuffles and moans of those around him. He thought of Alice at home in London and wondered how she would react when they told her. He tried to relive every moment they had spent together. Gradually, his conscious thoughts became indistinct and spiralled into a deep, pain-free sleep.

The sound of heavy rain dominated the dimly-lit ward when Jack awoke Friday morning. A doctor, he assumed, was unwinding the bandages that covered his face. When he opened his eyes, he could discern the blurred shapes of two figures hovering over him. *They look a little like the ears of a donkey*, he thought.

The doctor examined his burns and assured him that he would be right-as-rain in a few weeks.

"What about my eyes?" Jack asked.

"It's still too early to know," said the doctor, evasively. "They're badly damaged," he conceded, "but they will likely heal. Only time will tell."

Jack clung to the words, "likely heal," but the doctor's reply was not very comforting. An entry, made that day on Jack's Casualty Report Card MFW-42, read, "Wounded. Shell, Gas, Severe."

A second entry read, "Next of Kin Notified."

On Saturday morning, Miss Henderson chatted with Jack while she fed him a light breakfast; first a little apple juice, then warm oatmeal, and finally a few sips of tea. Jack asked her about the hospital and learned that it consisted of 24 huts and 36 tents. The buildings contained operating rooms, staff residences, a mess hall, offices and supplies. The tents were filled with beds for the wounded and dying. Miss Henderson told him how many other patients had arrived the day he was admitted, but she didn't mention that two of them died during the night.

Though the ever present burning persisted, Jack's pain was somewhat eased three times that day by the application of a cool, soothing solution of sodium bicarbonate. The rain ended during the night, and while the temperature remained in the low sixties, the sun shone periodically throughout the afternoon. Otherwise, the day was forgettable, though not for the 327 men who were being prepared for evacuation to England.

"When do you think they'll ship me home?" Jack asked as Miss Henderson put drops of medication in his eyes.

"Only the Army knows, and they don't tell *us* until it's time to get you ready."

Sunday dragged by without incident, aside from the death of another anonymous soldier in the tent next to Jack's. It rained throughout the day, and the patients huddled under their blankets in an effort to retain as much body heat as possible.

Jack awakened to a howling gale on Monday, and with steadily improving vision, looked up at the tightly stretched canvas overhead. The woven fabric was all that separated him and his fellow patients from the fury of the wind and a thorough drenching. The canvas alternately bulged and collapsed like a gigantic labouring lung while the support poles shuddered and swayed at the whim of the storm. The roaring wind and torrential rain battered the hospital with fury. The sheets, though warmed by Jack's body, felt damp, and his neck and face, especially his ears, were uncomfortably cold. He raised himself slightly on his elbows and looked about. Tightly packed rows of metal-framed cots stretched away in both directions, each occupied by a wounded soldier beneath a khaki blanket.

Two beds away, toward the tent's entrance, an officer whom Jack assumed to be a doctor, stood talking to a soldier who was sitting on the edge of his bed. The officer spoke in a subdued voice while a nursing sister, in a crisp white uniform, stood quietly at his side. The patient, still dressed in his battle-worn uniform didn't appear to be wounded though he was shaking as if suffering from severe hypothermia. His eyes were locked in a vacant stare, and he appeared to be trying desperately to speak though no words escaped lips. Jack heard only unintelligible stuttering sounds when the officer asked the man for the name of his next of kin. The soldier's efforts to reply seemed only to increase the involuntary trembling and twitching of his body. The man, struggling to control the movements of his hand and arm, reached into his tunic and withdrew a photo. Jack's eyesight was still far from normal, and he caught only a brief glimpse of the image, but he believed it was of a woman with something, perhaps a child, in her arms. The officer looked at the picture for a moment, turned it over briefly to examine the back, then returned it. He spoke quietly to the patient before producing a fountain pen and a notepad. Then he stood watching as the soldier struggled to write a few legible words.

The burns on Jack's thighs and testicles were still painful, and his body was weak and fatigued by his ordeal. He lowered himself back onto his cot, gathered the blanket to his chin to shut out the cold, and closed his eyes. He knew the soldier had experienced something unbearable, and he didn't want to think about it. Instead, he thought about Alice and wondered when he would see her again.

High winds and rain persisted through Tuesday and Wednesday, and Jack heard accounts of tents damaged and patients redistributed to accommodate the loss of more than 600 beds. Early Thursday morning he was awakened by Miss Henderson.

"Jack," she said, "Wake up. We have to get you ready to go."

"Go where?" Jack mumbled.

"To England," she said with a smile.

Within a couple of hours, Jack and 179 other casualties were loaded onto canvas stretchers and delivered to the nearby port. Then, one by one, they were carried aboard the *Ville-de-Liege*, a 1,500-ton screw steamer, commandeered in 1914 for transporting military personnel, especially those being evacuated from the Western Front.

CHAPTER THIRTEEN

ALICE'S SECRET

When the *Ville-de-Liege* docked in Folkestone Harbour, two burley orderlies carried Jack's stretcher down the gangplank, accompanied him to the station, and loaded him aboard a train for Bristol. He and a number of other gas casualties sped through the night to the city's Temple Meads Station, arriving early on the morning of August 31. He was transported to the Red Maids' Hospital, a 200-bed facility associated with Bristol's 2nd Southern General, where special equipment and expertise awaited victims of mustard gas attacks. Once treated and stabilized, gas casualties were destined to be redistributed to other hospitals throughout England.

The 5th Canadian Machine Gun Company fought on in France. At the end of each month, the company duty officer tallied up the numbers by which its contribution to the war was measured. Its official War Diary for the month of August reported three killed, sixteen wounded, and more than a half-million rounds of small arms ammunition expended; more than had been consumed in the four previous months. That cold statistic testified to the fierce fighting that Jack and his mates had faced at the Battle of Hill 70.

Jack's condition stabilized over the next few days. On September 12, he was transferred to the Canadian Convalescent Hospital at Bearwood in Berkshire, arriving the following day. His Medical Case Sheet described his injuries as a cough and burns to his left shoulder, testicles, thighs, left knee and right wrist. The hospital chaplain provided Jack with a current newspaper, as well as postcards and postage, so he could write to his family and friends. He quickly scribbled assurances to Canada and his brothers at the front that he was well and on the mend. Then he wrote to Alice with details of his whereabouts.

"I'm in bed 223D," wrote Jack, "There are thirty-six beds on the ward, and I'm just beyond halfway; on the left side as you enter the room."

He expressed his hope that she would come to visit him while he was there.

With her mother's approval, Alice missed the September 16th Sunday Service at Christ Church, Woburn Square in order to make the two-hour journey to Berkshire. As the train whisked her toward Wokingham, she re-read Jack's postcard and wondered in what condition she would find him. Though she had intended to be strong and positive for his sake, she began crying when she saw Jack lying in his bed. He was delighted to see her. He'd been in the army two years by then, and he'd had little interaction with loved ones aside from a few written words and occasional short leaves. Alice, with whom he had spent every leave since arriving in Britain, was his primary connection to the real world.

Jack took Alice's hand and reassured her, "It's alright, my dear. My eyes are much better, I'm not in pain, and the doctor says I'm doing well."

"I'm awfully glad to see you," he continued, "Please don't cry."

Immediately on being reunited, the couple's relationship moved beyond mutual infatuation. Even the ward nurses could see that they were in love.

The following day, Jack's brother, Frank, paid him an unexpected visit. The two compared their experiences at the front and reminisced about growing up in London. They recalled their adventures in Canada and traded tit-bits of family news. Then Jack told Frank all about Alice and their developing relationship. Eventually, the brothers said their goodbyes, and Frank started for the door.

"Don't forget," he said, looking over his shoulder, "when this is all over, you'll be returning to Canada."

A handwritten entry on Jack's Medical Case Sheet, dated the 26th of September, described his condition as "Fair, Cough improving." Two days later on Sunday afternoon, Jack was allowed to leave the ward for a few minutes to explore the hospital grounds with Alice.

"Be sure to have him back on the ward by half-three," demanded the head nurse.

"I will. I promise," assured Alice with a smile.

Alice visited Jack every Sunday during his thirty-day stay at Bearwood. Each time, she brought him a variety of little gifts, including apples, flowers, newspapers and a hair brush.

On October 13, 1917, fifty-two days after being carried out of the line near Lens, Private Collier was discharged from Bearwood and struck off the strength of the Canadian Machine Gun Depot. Over the next few weeks, his new unit, the 3rd Canadian Convalescent Depot at Seaford, subjected him to an endless series of medical examinations. Every detail of his condition was recorded on multiple copies of countless forms as the military bureaucracy prepared him for redeployment. But first, on Monday, the 15th of October, Jack was granted a fourteen-day convalescent leave. He threw his kit together and hurried to Seaford Station to board the train for London. There, he and Alice, now deeply in love with one another, spent every available moment together – *alone whenever possible.*

Each day throughout Jack's leave, Alice awaited the moment that the office clock struck 5 p.m. Then, she snatched up her purse and spilled out onto Regent Street to rush to the fountain in nearby Piccadilly Circus. There, each day, she found Jack waiting for her to fall into his open arms. Though the dreadful bombing of the city continued sporadically and battles still raged across the channel, Alice and Jack were distracted by their love for one another.

> When Zeppelin L45 released seven 300-pound bombs over London on the night of October 19, 1917, Mary Kingston, a widow of three years, returned to her home to find that, seven of her children had been killed. Edith (3 years old), Thomas (6), Richard (8), Kathleen (10), Mary (11), Bridget (16) and Annie (18) were buried five days later at Ladywell Cemetery. Mrs Kingston, overcome with grief and unable to walk, was carried to the graveside. The bomb that devastated her life was the last to be dropped on London by a Zeppelin in World War One.

In spite of Britain's shortage of butter, sugar, and flour, Rosina managed to surprise Jack with a small birthday cake on the evening before he returned to Seaford. His fortnight in London and the birthday celebration were a welcome respite from more than two years of military life.

On the 28th of October, three days prior to Jack's 23rd birthday, the inevitable end of their romantic fortnight arrived. The young lovers embraced one another in a quiet corner of a Victoria Station platform and lingered there until Jack's train began to move. Then, he quickly kissed his sweetheart one last time and turned to run after the moving train. Alice watched as he disappeared through the carriage door and didn't move until the last car of the train cleared the station amid a dense cloud of coal smoke.

When Alice left work on the 7th of December, a newsboy was shouting, "Canadian City in Ruins!" and holding up a copy of the paper for those passing by on Regent Street. Alice gave the boy a penny in exchange for a copy of the *Daily Express* and stood for a moment, reading the front-page story.

"The S. S. *Mont Blanc*, a French cargo ship," read Alice, "exploded in Halifax Harbour, Canada, after colliding with the Norwegian vessel, S. S. *Imo*."

"The Mont Blanc, laden with high explosives," continued the report, "was bound for France. The blast killed 1,782 people, injured 9,000, destroyed every structure within a half-mile radius of the ship, and was felt 130 miles away."

It seemed to Alice that reports of death and destruction were growing more incredible with each passing week. She read the final line of bold type, "The Mont Blanc's 90 mm deck gun landed 3½ miles from the explosion."

Then Alice folded the newspaper up. She would read the rest of the story as she rode home on the underground.

Ten days before Christmas, a medical board declared Jack "Fit for Duty."

"Happy Christmas" Jack muttered under his breath.

On December 15, a young soldier convalescing from wounds in Camiers, France, fell ill with a previously unknown respiratory disease. Eventually, it came to be known as the Spanish influenza. The virus spread throughout the world, killing in excess of 50 million people in 1918 and 1919, many of them soldiers who might otherwise have returned home when the war ended.

Two days after the medical board's decision, Canadian voters went to the polls to elect the 13th Parliament of Canada, and for the first time in history, the vast majority of women became eligible to vote. The mothers and sisters of those already at the front likely played a significant role in electing Sir Robert Borden's pro-conscription Unionist Party by a substantial majority.

The allied armies' insatiable appetite for soldiers continued to draw Canada's young men onto the battlefields of France.

Things were beginning to move quickly for Jack and, on December 21, 1917, he was reattached to the Canadian Machine Gun Depot. Then, though he felt more or less safe until after Christmas, he began his uncertain wait for re-assignment to the front.

Alice eagerly awaited Jack's Christmas leave. She was, on one hand, excited about seeing him and looked forward to their time together. On the other hand, she was terrified of sharing her secret with him; one she had kept to herself for almost a month. How would he react? What would he say? She wanted him to enjoy their Christmas holiday together and resolved to defer disclosing her surprise until the end of his visit.

Jack knocked at the door of 13 Coram Street and was greeted with a loving embrace and a tender kiss. Rosina, pleased to see her daughter happy and full of enthusiasm for life, stood behind her, waiting to welcome Jack to their home.

"Peter works at the hotel until nine," Rosina explained, "so supper will be quite late. Would you like a bowl of hot soup to tide you over?"

"No thank you, Mrs Geherty," he returned.

"A cup of tea then, and an oat cake?" she offered.

"Yes, thank you. A cup of tea would be nice," said Jack.

To Alice, it seemed Jack's time in London always passed too quickly, and yet the intervals between dragged on and on. Before she knew it, his leave was nearing its end.

"Jack Dear," said Alice as he was packing the last of his kit, "Can we leave for the station a little early today? I'd like to spend some time with you – alone."

"Yes, of course, Alice," replied Jack.

A little over an hour later, Alice and her beau sat close together on a bench in St. James's Park, a short walk from Victoria Station. Alice shivered, and Jack wondered why she chose to linger in the park on such a bitter winter day. The wind tore at their clothing and seeped inside, stealing the warmth from their bodies. The war, though never far from the consciousness of anyone in London, was no longer Alice's prime concern. She was clearly upset, but Jack thought little of it in light of the fact that they were about to be separated for what might turn out to be months. He reassured her that he'd likely visit again before returning to France, but instead of replying, she looked away. When she turned back, Alice looked directly into Jack's eyes. A tear trickled crookedly down her cheek.

"Oh Jack," she began, pausing as if searching for a word, "I'm going to have a baby," she whispered, and fell into his arms.

Jack held her, said nothing for a moment, and embarked on his own search for words.

"Alice," he began, "don't cry, my dear. I'll . . . when is the baby . . . I'll marry you. We'll get married."

"Oh, Jack!" sobbed Alice.

Within two days of returning to the Canadian Machine Gun Depot at Seaford, Jack met with the chaplain and made arrangements to rescind his assignment of pay to his father. Instead, half of his pay, fifteen dollars per month, would go directly to Alice effective January 1. Then, he began the process of applying to the depot commander for permission to marry. The chaplain warned Jack that the procedure was complicated and likely to take a long time, but he promised to do everything possible to expedite the paperwork.

Jack wrote a letter to his mother, announcing his intention to marry Alice Geherty, the London-born daughter of a hotel maître d'. He had talked about her in previous letters but had shared few details of their relationship. Deliberately avoiding any mention of Alice's condition, he told his mum how anxious he was that she meet Alice when the war was over.

The Canadian Machine Gun Depot's 1918 New Year celebration was a half-hearted affair. Those who had been unable to arrange leave, including Jack, listened to a few words from their Commanding Officer, enjoyed some light non-alcoholic refreshments, and joined in the singing of a few popular songs before lights out.

Jack was summoned by Lieutenant Waddington on the 1st of February.

"Finally!" Jack thought to himself as he wiped the toes of his boots, one after the other, on his puttee-wrapped calves. He entered the Lieutenant's office, saluted and stood at attention.

"At ease, Collier," began the subaltern, "I'm sure you're eager to get back to France, so I'll get right to it. You've been reassigned to the Canadian Engineers Training Depot. Get your kit sorted and be prepared to report tomorrow at zero-seven-hundred-hours. Good luck Private. That is all."

Jack, completely caught off guard, came to attention, saluted and about-faced. He was ill-prepared for this sudden change of circumstances. He had naively expected the lieutenant to announce approval of his request to marry. Instead, he found himself a step closer to the front and farther away from Alice. His head was spinning with thoughts of his sweetheart, his return to France, and the impact that his re-assignment would have on his application to marry. He made repeated enquiries through the chaplain's office over the next three and a half months while undergoing additional training.

On the 22nd of May, Alice, now seven months pregnant, received a postcard in the morning post. It read, in part, "I've been posted to the 2nd Canadian Engineers Reinforcement Battalion. No word on the other yet."

Things happened quickly after that.

In June, the Chaplain advised Jack that his application for permission to marry had been approved, but that he would need to hurry if he wanted to get married before being re-deployed. Jack arranged an emergency leave with his commander, notified Alice, and set out for London.

Nineteen-year-old Alice Rose Geherty and Private John Albert Collier were married at Christ Church, Woburn Square on the 15th of June, 1918. They had only hours to celebrate the most important event of Alice's life before Jack kissed her goodbye and returned to Seaford Camp.

Eight days later, on Alice's twentieth birthday, her husband was assigned to the Engineers Reinforcement Pool in France, marking the beginning of his second combat deployment. By virtue of his attachment to the Engineers, his rank changed from private to "sapper." Jack arrived in France the following day, but he didn't join his unit until the 3rd of July when, as one of seventy reinforcements, he reported to the 11th Battalion Canadian Engineers' headquarters at Burbure, France. Just ten miles to the south-east of the village was the Noeux-Les-Mines dressing station where he had been taken after being gassed the previous summer.

The young Collier found himself "in the thick of it" almost immediately, when the day after his arrival, Burbure was subjected to heavy shelling throughout the night.

CHAPTER FOURTEEN

BELGIUM BOUND

On Saturday, July 6, 1918, the 11th Battalion Canadian Engineers moved from Burbure, France to billets at Hurionville, a mile away. Then, on Tuesday, they marched three miles southward to Auchel for baths. By Wednesday morning they had set out for Madagascar Corners, a twenty-mile march to the south. There, two miles from the city of Arras, the Canadians relieved the British Royal Engineers' 400th Field Company. Over the next three weeks they undertook the construction of six dug-outs and assumed the repair and maintenance of two dozen forward and support trenches in the area. Jack's job, as a machine gunner, was to provide cover for them while they worked.

On the 25th of July, two weeks after Jack's arrival at Madagascar Corners, Alice gave birth to their daughter. The baby was registered with three names. The first two honoured Alice's schoolmates, now her sisters-in-law, *Constance* and *Violet*. The third, *Rose*, was Alice's middle name as well as the name most commonly used by her mother, Rosina.

Alice wrote to Jack with the exciting news on the morning after the baby's birth. She was disappointed that her husband wasn't able to be there to hold their new-born though she was pleased to have the support of her parents and her London friends while he was at the front. That was not to be the case when, years later in Canada, her other four children were born.

In her letter, Alice included the news that Jack's brother, Frank, who had been wounded in early April, had been discharged from 1st Birmingham War Hospital and posted to Woodcote Park, a Canadian convalescent hospital at Epson. She knew how much her husband worried about his brothers, and she understood how such bits of news were appreciated by those on the continent.

On the 31st of July, Jack's unit was relieved by the 412th Royal Engineers. They remained at Madagascar Corners for another three days, then at 7:45 p.m. on August 3, the men of the 11th boarded lorries for an unknown destination. As the convoy bumped slowly along deeply rutted dirt roads over

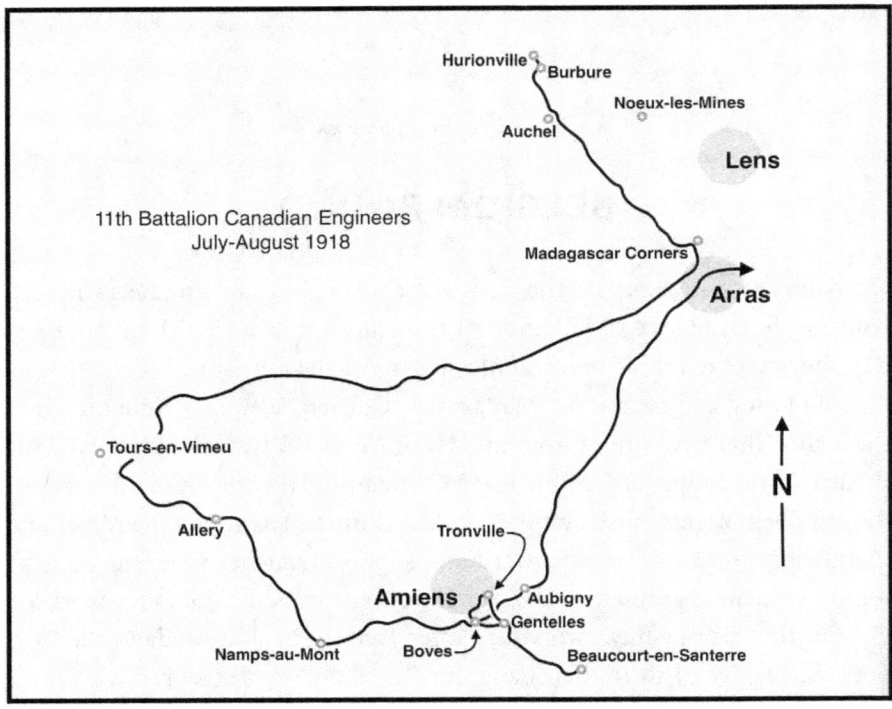

Movements of the 11th Battalion, Canadian Engineers between 6 July and 29 August 1918.

the next twelve hours, Jack began to sense that something was up, and he was right. While those designated as "other ranks" were kept in the dark, the commanders of all four divisions of the Canadian Corps were secretly assembling their men in preparation for the Battle of Amiens. It was to be the first offensive in what became known as the "Hundred Days Campaign" which was to continue until Armistice Day on the 11th of November. When Jack and the others disembarked from the lorries, they found themselves more than fifty miles to the west of Arras, five miles outside of Tours-en-Vimeu. In the early morning light, after hours of bouncing around in the backs of lorries with little sleep, they proceeded in column formation to their billets, arriving at 10 a.m. on the fourth of August.

To the men in the ranks, being transported so far west of the front made little sense. What they didn't know at the time was that large numbers of personnel were converging on Amiens by circuitous routes in an effort to maintain the element of surprise. The 11th Battalion, at the most westerly point of its journey near Tours-en-Vimeu, was about to turn east again. The engineers rested throughout the day, ate supper, and paraded just prior to 9 p.m. Then, they set off once more; *by the left, quick, march*! Ten miles later, at 4 a.m. on the 5th of August, they arrived at the village of Allery. Jack and his comrades managed a few hours of precious rest before the order was given to "fall in" at 11 p.m. Sixteen miles of "very bad roads" lead the column of engineers to Namps-au-Mont where they arrived at 10:30 a.m. on the 6th of August.

"Where the Hell are we going?" Jack asked no one in particular.

"What I want to know is *when* are we going to get there?" came the response from someone down the line.

Another day of rest, followed by yet another fifteen-mile night march saw Jack and his mates bivouacked in Boves Wood shortly after 6 a.m. The night marches were taking their toll in the form of minor injuries. One member of D Company, was unable to walk after stumbling in the dark and twisting his ankle. He was admitted to the Canadian Field Ambulance to recover before re-joining the battalion a few days later. It was clear to everyone that the night marches were designed to hide their movements from the enemy, and they could feel the tension in the air. Though most didn't know it at the time, the battalion had already reached the concentration area southeast of Amiens.

The following night was a "piece of cake," a mere four-mile hike to Tronville Wood with frequent breaks along the way. The engineers were briefed and started out at 10 p.m. arriving at two in the morning on the eighth. Jack calculated he and his crew had hauled the Vickers Mark I limber about forty-five miles in four nights. Though the long night marches had come to an end for the time being, he knew that every end was simply the *beginning* of something different.

Two hours and twenty minutes after Jack arrived at Tronville Wood, 900 Allied field guns opened fire, and the Canadian infantry advanced into the Battle of Amiens behind a creeping barrage. It was 4:20 a.m. on the 8th of August, and the engineers followed the infantry onto the battlefield. The Germans were not prepared for the scale of the assault and fell back. Many of them were overrun and surrendered during the three-day battle. It quickly became Germany's greatest defeat since the beginning of the war.

Jack's unit was on the move again though no longer in column formation in the dark. Exhausted, a condition with which they were all too familiar, the engineers reached Beaucourt-en-Santerre by three-thirty in the afternoon. While the Battle of Amiens raged on around them, they repaired roads and made a reconnaissance of cellar accommodations and wells in the area. They searched for booby-traps left behind by retreating enemy forces, tested water for poisons, and cleared rubble from buildings to provide shelter for the infantry behind the line. All the while, Jack and his machine gun watched over them.

> *The Manchester Guardian*, 10 August 1918
> "It is a great victory. The 2nd German Army has suffered a humiliating reverse, the extent of which, even yet, cannot be fully estimated, and much of its organisation which covered the open country before Amiens has been, for the moment at least, practically destroyed. I do not think that war has ever yielded such extraordinary stories of rout and the confusion of trained soldiers. General von der Marwitz no longer has Amiens by the throat. It is doubtful whether he has any kind of grip on his own bewildered men."

On August 10, Jack guarded a work detail whose task it was to bury fifteen recently killed horses. It was a major undertaking, carried out entirely by hand with shovels, but it was essential to prevent the spread of disease. In spite of such efforts, the stench of death was never far away, and the pungent odour triggered memories among the war's veterans for decades afterward.

The following night, two men died when the camp was shelled, and nine others were wounded. Seven of the battalion's horses were killed and eleven more were injured before the three-day battle ended.

In the wake of the allied advance, Jack spent much of the rest of August protecting those who repaired the roads, posted signs, dug wells, established water points and installed storage tanks and troughs for horses.

At 8:40 p.m. on August 24, the 11th Battalion Canadian Engineers set out from Beaucourt-en-Santerre for Gentelles Wood, about eight miles away. The column was shelled near Cayeux while en route, but it arrived at 2 a.m. the following morning without casualties. The men bivouacked there for three days, maintaining trenches and dugouts, cutting fire steps into front line trenches, burying horses, and stringing coils of barbed wire in front of the trenches at night.

In the meantime, about forty miles to the northwest of Jack's location, the Canadian Corps launched the Battle of the Scarpe, named for the river valley east of Arras. The offensive's objective was to pursue the German Army as it retreated eastward through the Scarpe Valley and then capture the enemy-held Drocourt-Quéant Line, a substantial enemy trench system between the town of Drocourt in the north and Quéant to the south. The next objective was to take Canal du Nord which lay further to the east. Before the four-day battle ended, the Canadians captured fifty-three artillery pieces, recovered more than 500 machine guns, and took 3,300 prisoners, but the price of victory was 5,800 casualties. In spite of their losses, and an unusually heavy rain on August 27, the Canadians pressed on.

Engineers were essential to the infantry's eastward advance, so at 6:30 a.m. on the morning of the twenty-eighth, the men of the 11th moved off from Gentelles Wood to Boves Station where they entrained for Aubigny. It was 1:30 a.m. when Jack disembarked and clambered into a lorry for the thirty-five-mile ride to Arras. Eleven hours after setting out from Gentelles Wood, the battalion settled into bivouac in the fields and trenches east of Arras.

In London, Alice scanned the lists of casualties in the daily newspapers and diligently followed the progress of the war. It was a difficult pursuit as most reports were days old by the time they appeared in print, and all were meticulously censored. While British and French-led battles dominated the headlines, reports of the Canadian Corps' accomplishments and casualties were scant, relatively brief, and generally buried deep within the papers' rearmost pages.

On the 2nd of September at 5 a.m. the Canadian Corps launched another attack behind a creeping barrage, a tactic which had first proved successful at Vimy Ridge the previous year. The coveted Drocourt-Quéant Line soon came under the control of the Canadians. Immediately, the engineers moved into the captured area to take up their assigned positions and carry out their customary support duties under fire. Jack and his team watched over them like a shepherd overseeing his flock, while they repaired roads, erected signs and established water points.

By the end of the 4th of September, four more engineers had been killed, and two of their officers and eighteen other ranks had been wounded. The

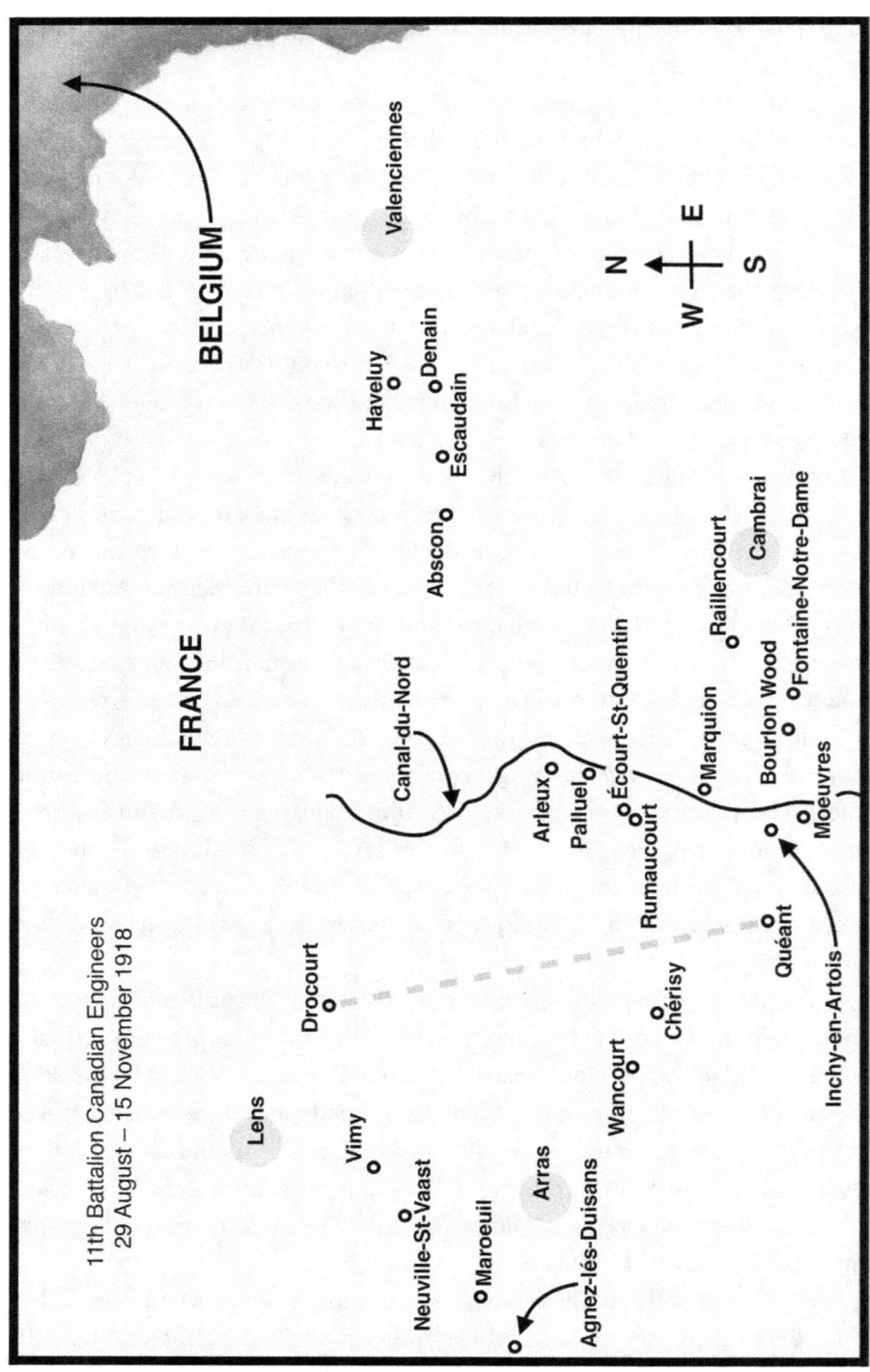

fighting continued over the next fortnight while the German Army slowly retreated eastward. Jack's fellow sappers spent several days rebuilding the bridge over Le Cojeul, a small river at Wancourt, before moving on toward Chérisy. For the first time, Jack dared to hope that the allies were winning the war.

At home, Alice took baby Connie to Christ Church, Woburn Square to be baptised and wished Jack could have been there with her. She hadn't heard from her husband for almost two weeks and worried that something unthinkable had happened to him. In that, she was not alone as hundreds of thousands of Allied wives checked the post regularly for letters and postcards from their men. During the Great War, news of casualties came to loved ones in the form of a telegram from the War Office. They customarily began with, "It is with deepest regret that I inform you ..." or "It is my painful duty to inform you ..." Mothers and wives were consumed with terror every time they saw a telegram delivery boy pedal his bicycle onto their street. Most held their breath until the dreaded cyclist had passed by their door. When he didn't, some slumped to their knees and wept, without even having read the telegram.

On the nineteenth, the 11th Battalion rested and bathed. Jack took advantage of the opportunity to write to Alice. He signed "With love, to you and Baby" and gave the unsealed letter to Lieutenant Wylie to pass on to the field post office. Britain's Army Postal Service censored all outgoing mail, to ensure that it contained nothing related to military operations. Jack could not tell Alice where he was or make any reference to his current duties.

Bags of mail addressed to military personnel being processed at the Regents Park sorting facility.

While the army recognized the risks that security breaches posed to allied operations, it understood that mail was critical to the morale of its soldiers and those at home. It made every effort to deliver letters to the front within two days of being posted in Britain. As one might expect, the volume of mail addressed to military personnel in war-time was enormous.

Shortly after the war began, Britain's General Post Office erected a massive wooden structure in London's Regents Park. It housed sorting operations for mail addressed to military personnel and employed 2,500 workers, most of whom were sorters. At the height of the conflict, allied soldiers received as many as twelve million letters and postcards *each week*.

On the 20th of September, the men of *The Eleventh* were issued clean uniforms. Then they paraded for inspection of their gas masks, weapons, and other issued equipment before resuming their eastward advance. By late September, they had passed through Quéant at the southern extreme of the Drocourt-Quéant Line and arrived in Inchy-en-Artois just west of the Canal-Du-Nord. On the 27th, the fourth Canadian Division crossed the canal and advanced to Fontaine-Notre-Dame east of Bourlon Wood. Over the next ten days, Jack and his comrades carried out their specialized duties over an area from Inchy-en-Artois and Moeuvres, west of the canal, to Fontaine-Notre-Dame and Raillencourt, east of it.

By the end of September, another six of Jack's fellow engineers had been evacuated to field hospitals due to wounds.

Then, the battalion was taken out of the line and transported to Maroeuil north-west of Arras. The convoy of lorries arrived at 5:30 a.m. on the 7th of October, and the men ate breakfast and slept for most of the day. Kit inspections, clothing parades, training and organized sports kept them busy until Sunday, October 13 when they attended church parade followed by pay parade. Though no one yet knew it, the armistice was less than a month away when at 7:30 a.m. on the fourteenth, they climbed into the backs of lorries for the journey to the Agnes–les–Duisans rail station. There, they boarded railway carriages which carried them to Marquion, slightly east of Canal-du-Nord.

Jack had little understanding of the geography of France as he moved through its eastern towns and villages. There were few notable landmarks and every point of departure and destination looked alike. After all, the landscape along the roads and rail lines had been sliced up by trenches and torn to pieces by shells. Every village was shattered beyond recognition and signs had been torn down by retreating armies. Jack quickly forgot the names of most communities as he passed from one to another. Only those in which he remained for an extended period lingered in his memory after the war.

On the 15th of the month, the battalion arrived in Rumacourt and began improving roads, repairing damaged bridges and constructing new ones in the area. The 11th Battalion's October war diary read like a gazetteer as its personnel followed the retreating enemy through France toward Belgium. 'D' Company restored bridges on the Écourt-St.-Quentin to Arleux Road and between Palluel and Arleux; 'A' Company worked on the roads around Rumacourt and at Abscon; 'B' Company moved to Haveluy where they too worked at road repairs; and 'C' Company was assigned to Bellevue and Escaudain.

By October 31, Jack Collier's twenty-fourth birthday, the 11th Battalion was on the outskirts of Valenciennes, where it established its headquarters three days later. There, just eight miles from the Belgian boarder and eight days before the war ended, Captain Hay, Lieutenant Miller and an unnamed sapper were gassed and evacuated from the line.

Jack was no longer the young man who had kissed his mother goodbye in the spring of 1916. He had endured bombardments, endless fatigue, cold and incessant rain, and the loss of men with whom he had shared long nights and tepid tea. He had withstood the test of combat and had survived. He'd seen and felt things he would never forget. Though still small of stature, he was strong, capable and confident. He was invincible!

Rumours abounded in London. The German Army was collapsing, and surely the end of the war was near. Alice was growing hopeful that she and her husband would soon be reunited. She had been a carefree teenager when they met in 1916. Though still pretty and filled with enthusiasm for life, she too had changed since the declaration of war. The continuous worry and moments of intense fear had chipped away at her idealism, but she remained optimistic. By November of 1918, she had become a mother and a wife with a greatly altered perspective, in part because she had witnessed the world's dark side.

On the 11th of November, 1918, Lieutenant Robert Duff Kinmond, a recipient of the Military Cross, wrote in the 11th Battalion Canadian Engineers' War Diary, "Hostilities ceased at 1100 hours, no great demonstrations. Massed bands played in the square [Valenciennes] for 10 minutes."

The following day, three of the battalion's companies worked on repairing local roads while the fourth, 'D' Company, supervised the construction of a firing range. The Canadian Expeditionary Force consisted of a quarter of a million men, and it would take several months to organize and execute their repatriation to Canada. In the mean time, they had to be billeted somewhere, fed, clothed and kept busy while they waited.

Jack Collier, along with the 11th Battalion Canadian Engineers crossed the border into Belgium on the 16th of November and spent the winter of 1918 and 1919 there. Throughout the remainder of the month, they were garrisoned in Dour and Frameries, where their days were occupied with inspections, equipment maintenance, drill, sports, and weekly church parades.

In the first week of December, the battalion's officers kept the men occupied with physical training and sports, but in the second week they marched them through Givry to Binche; then through Morlanwelz, Chapelle-lez-Herlaimont, Courcelles and Gosselies to Ransart. By the 17th of the month, they had passed through Fleurus, Gembloux and Orbais to Gistoux, where they remained until the 3rd of May 1919.

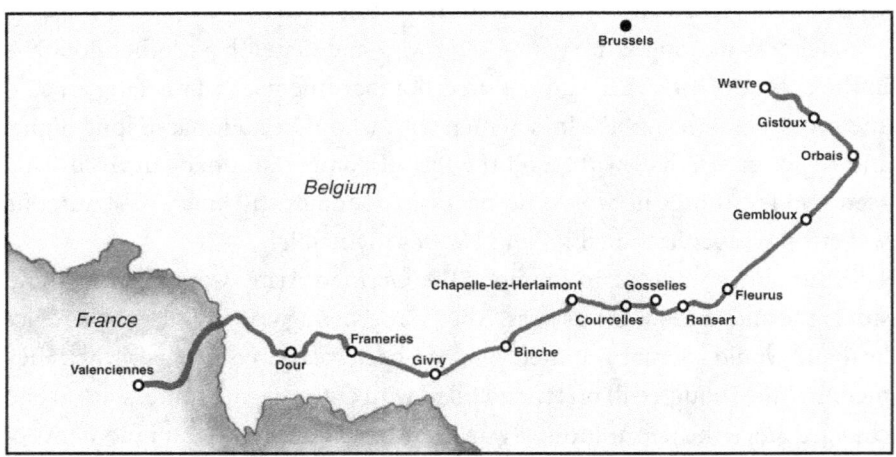

Movements of the 11th Battalion, Canadian Engineers between 31 October 1918 and 3 May 1919.

For Jack, just one of thousands of Canadian soldiers awaiting repatriation, it was a long and dreary winter. He was fed up with military life, but more importantly, he was anxious to see his wife and baby Connie in London, and eager to get home to his family in Hamilton. Everyone in uniform just wanted to resume their lives among familiar surroundings.

Sapper Collier was granted a fortnight's leave to the United Kingdom on the 29th of March. He could barely contain his excitement at the prospect of seeing Alice again and meeting his eight-month-old daughter for the first time. He had been in France and Belgium for more than ten months and had watched others go on leave and return with stories of their time in England.

He and Alice cherished every minute of his fourteen-days of freedom and made plans for their lives together in Canada. Their second child, another daughter, was conceived during this leave.

Jack, according to his military record, re-joined his unit at Gistoux, Belgium on the 14th of April, 1919, but his ordeal was nearing its end. At 2:30 p.m. on May 3, 1919, the men of the 11th formed up in columns of three to march to Wavre, where they entrained at 6:00 p.m. They detrained at 8:45 p.m. on the fourth, almost twenty-seven hours later, and were marched to the embarkation camp in the coastal port of Le Havre, France. By then, everyone was rather critical of the military's travel arrangements, but their officers responded to their complaints with, "You should be happy we didn't make you march all the way."

Though tired and frustrated with military bureaucracy, the men of The 11th were happy to have finally begun their journey home. They were deloused and put through baths the following day.

Five days after arriving at La Havre, the engineers sailed to Southampton. By noon on the 10th, they had moved into their barracks at Milford Camp, one of four camps at Witley, England. Over the next three days the men were mustered and examined by doctors and dentists. Then, on May 15th, the entire battalion, Jack included, went on leave for ten days.

On his return to camp, Jack began filling out the paperwork essential to his repatriation, his final pay entitlements, and his eventual release from service. He and his comrades were presented with a forty-eight-page booklet titled, "Canada and Her Soldiers." It contained a statement of gratitude for their service and information about the repatriation process. The majority of his mates were scheduled to sail for Canada on the 7th of June, but because he had married while overseas, he would have to wait a little longer.

Vessels designated "dependent ships" were being contracted to carry soldiers and their families to Canada, but that would take another two or three months to organize. With their processing complete, the battalion went on leave again on May 28th.

CHAPTER FIFTEEN

TEN DAYS AT SEA

The brutality of the Great War was evident by the monuments left in its wake. Abandoned military equipment, unexploded shells and fresh graves littered the fields of Europe. Trenches and craters scarred the landscape. Ancient villages, reduced to heaps of bricks and mortar, attested to four years of inhumanity. Shattered glass and splintered wood testified to the mayhem of battle. Most apparent in Great Britain were the absences; the food shortages, missing limbs, and empty chairs at dining room tables.

In addition to being brutalised by the war, the world was victimised by a fatal influenza. It first appeared in the fall of 1917 at Etaples, the staging camp and military hospital complex in France through which Jack had passed as he entered and later exited the battlefield. While doctors understood the roll of bacteria in the spread of diseases, viruses were still unknown to medical science. They were simply too small to be seen with an optical microscope. Consequently, airborne viruses were much harder to understand and manage, and because the pandemic appeared during war-time, governments supressed information about the virus's severity and the number of its victims. The unprecedented movement of troops between continents accelerated the spread of the illness. In the pre-radio era, when the public relied on newspapers for information, news travelled more slowly. Many became fully aware of the threat only after it had established a foothold in their community; sometimes within their families. Post-war reports claimed that a half-million German soldiers died after contracting influenza. The pandemic swept through Europe and around the globe, killing infants, parents and grandparents with equal indifference. Almost three per cent of the world's population, an estimated fifty million people, died from what became known as the Spanish flu.

Groups of little girls could be heard singing a new chant as they turned their skipping ropes:

"I had a little bird.
Its name was Enza.
I opened the window
And INFLUENZA."

Neither Alice's, nor Jack's family suffered a loss to the influenza, but as the date of their passage approached, they became concerned about newspaper reports of outbreaks aboard ships bound for Canada.

Nevertheless, "the War to end all wars" was over, and each day brought new hope to those who had endured so much for so long. Wonderful things were happening in medicine, and new technologies were beginning to appear. A week prior to Alice's twenty-first birthday, she and thousands of others lined the streets of London to welcome British aviators, Captain John Alcock and Lieutenant Arthur Brown, to the city. The pair had just completed the world's first non-stop trans-Atlantic flight. They had set out from Newfoundland in their twin-engine, open-cockpit, bi-plane at 1:45 p.m. on June 14 and crash landed in the Derrygimlagh Bog near Clifden in County Galway at 8:40 a.m. the following day. As they passed by Alice in an open car surrounded by a throng of admirers, she took a photo of the pair with an early Kodak Brownie box camera.

The demobilization and repatriation of more than 267,000 troops along with their 54,000 dependents was an enormous logistical challenge. By August, Jack had waited almost nine months since the Armistice of November 11, 1918. Less than a week before boarding the R.M.S. *Corsican*, Jack looked on as Captain W. H. Draper stamped his demobilization order with a blue oval imprint. It read, "Canadian Discharge Depot, C.E.F. Buxton, Derbyshire – August 2 1919." His battalion had sailed out of Halifax Harbour more than thirty-eight months earlier. So much had happened since then. He'd endured almost a year of training in England, survived the horrors of the battlefield twice, and fallen in love. Now, finally, he was returning to his pre-war home, memories of which seemed almost dream-like.

Three days earlier on July 30, Alice received an official-looking letter in the post and held her breath as she opened it. The pre-printed return address indicated it had come from the Department of Immigration and Colonisation. The letter advised that she and her daughter would be sailing from Liverpool on the 8th of August, aboard the *Corsican*, along with Jack.

Immediately, Alice recalled reading an obscure little article in *The Times* a couple of months earlier. It described the experiences of soldier's wives travelling to Canada and quoted the January 9 edition of the *Calgary Daily Herald*. The paper's headline read, "Rats Drive Women Up on Decks. Women Afraid to Go Down to Their Berths." Though she had never been to sea, she had heard her father's account of sailing to America in 1893 more than once while she was growing up. The experience had been an exciting adventure from his perspective, and Alice was looking forward to her passage with some enthusiasm. Still, from time to time, she thought about the rats, the Spanish flu, and the sinking of the *Titanic*, but Jack's assurances kept her from dwelling on her fears.

"Don't fret Alice," he reasoned, "I've sailed to Canada and back without a bit of trouble, and ships are setting out to cross the ocean every day now. We'll be fine. I'm sure of it."

"And," he lied, "I never saw rats on either crossing."

The Canadian Government's Repatriation Committee provided Alice with a booklet titled, "Information for Wives of Soldiers Coming from Overseas." The publication explained that soldiers' wives and children were entitled to third-class accommodation aboard the ship to which they were assigned. Train fare from their current address to the port of embarkation, and fares to their final destination in Canada, were also funded by the Canadian Government. Throughout the journey, however, travellers would be responsible for the cost of their meals and personal needs. London's war-brides were directed to the Emigration Office at 11–12 Charing Cross to secure their travel orders. Thereafter, the pamphlet dealt with what to expect in Canada. It advised war-brides to pack warm stockings, rubbers, goloshes, a sweater and a hat. Then it went on to describe Canadian summers as "delightful." The booklet left a lot of questions unanswered, but Alice was confident that Jack would provide the answers when the time came.

In addition to the "rats" story, Alice heard some pretty disparaging tales about third-class ship-board accommodations, and her father urged her to enquire about booking a cabin when she went to the Emigration Office.

"How much will it cost me to book a second-class cabin?" asked Alice.

"There's a shortage of cabins on these ships, mum," replied the official, "If you wish to book one, you'll not set foot in Canada before November, I wager."

Alice was disappointed, but she wasn't about to sail to Canada on her own, months after Jack's scheduled return.

"Never mind then," she conceded.

England's police constables had been seeking better wages and pensions for more than forty years prior to the summer of 1919. With war news no longer dominating the front pages of the papers, their demands were attracting a lot of attention. The police union called for a national strike on Friday, August 1, and London's *Daily Herald*, eager to report the story ahead of its competitors, took a calculated risk. The paper's early edition, published in the pre-dawn darkness, included accounts of a "widespread strike" in the capital though there were still hours to go before the strike was to begin. The London police strike didn't materialize, but the *Herald* was already on the train, speeding toward Liverpool. When it arrived, half of the city's police responded to the story by failing to report for duty. They weren't the only Scousers who read the paper. As darkness enveloped the city, bands of unruly looters began breaking shop windows and helping themselves to booty. When the sun rose on Saturday morning, Liverpool's streets were littered with broken glass and abandoned remnants of stolen merchandise. The situation worsened when, on Saturday, even fewer constables reported for work. On the 4th of August, the *Liverpool Daily Post* described the lawlessness as "an orgy of looting and rioting." Finally, after three days of chaos, the British Army was summoned to the city to restore order. War-hardened soldiers fixed bayonets to their rifles and fired a volley of shots over the rioters' heads. By the end of the week, confrontations with the army and those constables who remained on duty left several dead, hundreds injured, and 200 charged with looting. The 1919 Liverpool riots were among Alice's last memories of her beloved England.

Jack was mustered for departure from the United Kingdom at 4 a.m. on the 8th of August. He stood by with his kit, awaiting the order that was to begin his return journey to Canada. The shrill of a whistle marked the moment it began.

"We passed through the gates of Witley Camp at 4:30 a.m," recalled Jack, "and entrained at Witley station."

"We were all pretty excited at first," he continued, "but after a while everyone got real quiet. I guess we were all thinking of our mums and dads, and what it was going to be like when we got home. We got off the train in

Liverpool, marched to the docks and boarded the *Corsican*, embarking about 5 p.m."

Alice's life had already changed dramatically since meeting Jack, but on Friday, August 8, 1919, her future was irrevocably altered when she stepped from Liverpool's Princess Landing Stage onto the gangway of the R.M.S. *Corsican*. Baby Connie, eyes closed and completely oblivious to the significance of the event, barely noticed the familiar rocking motion as Alice carried her up the steep

Troops boarding the ship that was to carry them home to their families.

ramp. The infant dozed comfortably in her mother's arms, unaware that she was the last of her line to be born on the eastern side of the Atlantic. The procession of third-class passengers stepped one after the other onto the ship's thickly painted deck and proceeded to a small wooden desk behind which sat the *Corsican*'s purser.

"May I see your ticket ma'am?" asked the purser.

"Yes, of course," Alice replied, holding out the documents provided by the Emigration Office.

On page fifteen of the ship's manifest, beneath the heading "dependents," was a growing hand-written list of third-class passengers. On line "28" the purser wrote "Alice Collier" and "child" in the appropriate columns. The young mother looked about as he wrote. She was somewhat bewildered by the unfamiliar surroundings, but within a few minutes she had been guided, first this way and then that, toward her assigned deck. Her initial impression of the ship was that it was cold, hard and stiff. There was no holiday atmosphere to be found aboard and no evidence of glamour, past or present. She was directed to the orlop deck, the lowest of all the decks, well below the waterline. There, in a large and otherwise empty area, she was assigned to one of dozens of two-level berths arranged in rows and separated by canvas curtains. Dim electric lights protruded out of the deckhead at intervals, creating dark shadows and offering minimal light. No provisions had been made for infants such as Connie. She and her mother would have to share the narrow lower berth throughout the voyage. The sight of utilitarian berths in cramped quarters with limited privacy was disappointing, but Alice resolved to make the best of the situation. After all, she couldn't do anything to change it, and it was just for a week or so. With a sigh of resignation, she sat down on her berth and looked about. Through the soles of her shoes, she felt the vibrations of the ship's engines and knew she would likely be at sea within the hour. Travel weary and more than four months pregnant with her second child, she held her sleeping daughter tenderly and looked on as those around her settled in. A lone tear emerged from the corner of her eye and sparkled in the yellow artificial light as it trickled down her cheek. She already missed her mum and dad terribly.

R.M.S. Corsican, *a so-called "dependent ship"*

The 500-foot *Corsican*, built twelve years earlier in Glasgow, was operated by Canadian Pacific Ocean Services in 1919. She was designated a "dependent ship," contracted by the military to return soldiers and their families to Canada. Some war-brides have since described their accommodations as overcrowded, dirty and suffering from a lack of amenities. A contemporary Canadian newspaper quoted one soldier's wife as saying, "The conditions below were so repulsive that we could not stand it, and had to spend the time on deck, where there were no chairs, and nothing but the mouldy, dirty deck to sit on."

The troops had already boarded and were berthed on a different deck than their dependents, but families were permitted to meet on a common deck each morning to spend the day and eat their meals together. Weather permitting, they wandered about the deck together, participated in activities organized by a YMCA representative, and visited with other families. Nightly dances, held on deck "C" throughout the passage, were among the most popular ship-board activities, but there were church services, lectures, sing-alongs and games as well.

Still, the Canadian military's policy of berthing troops in separate quarters from their families meant Alice was on her own for almost half of the time that she was aboard the ship. Sometimes, awakened by the relentless cries of babies in the night, she felt very alone and vulnerable.

Each of the next ten days drew Alice deeper into exile; further from friends and family. Never again would she feel the warmth of her father's hugs. Never again would she hear her mother's voice. Neither she, nor her young husband could realistically expect to see England again. It was simply an economic impossibility, but surely somewhere in her heart, she must have hoped to return some day.

The ship sailed northward through the Irish Sea and turned westward around the seventy-five-foot-high Inishtrahull Light off the northern coast of Ireland. Then it followed a great-circle route through the vast emptiness of the Atlantic until the Belle Isle light came into view. Because it was a summer passage and the St. Lawrence River was free of ice, the ship's destination was Quebec City.

Though Alice felt a little queasy on the morning of August 9, she quickly brushed her hair and dressed, so she could be on "C" Deck when Jack arrived. Instead, she found him waiting at the top of the companionway. They embraced and immediately made their way to breakfast. A sea breeze tugged at baby Connie's blanket as they walked, and waves slapped noisily against the ship's hull. Years later, Alice recalled that most days were sunny and pleasant, but the wind was harsh on the exposed deck. While her berth offered protection from the elements at the end of each day, being alone rekindled thoughts of her family and friends in London. Sometimes she sobbed herself to sleep.

On Alice's third day at sea, she was trying to get dressed for breakfast, but little Connie was fussy and demanding her attention. The woman who occupied the berth across the aisle offered to hold the baby while Alice got ready. She introduced herself as May Harrison from England's Midlands.

"I heard you telling the purser you are going to Hamilton," said Mrs Harrison.

"Yes, my husband's family lives there," Alice admitted.

"My Bill and I are going there as well."

"Oh," responded Alice, "then you'll be taking the train too; from Quebec I mean."

"Yes, perhaps we'll see one another on the train."

The two war-brides soon became friends and introduced their husbands to one another. Though Bill Harrison, a member of Hamilton's 36th Battalion, and Jack Collier had never met, their British heritage, military experiences, and connection to Hamilton gave them lots to talk about. The couples enjoyed one another's company and remained close friends throughout their lives.

As Alice and Jack said goodnight at the end of their fifth day at sea, the *Corsican* entered the summer iceberg limit at about thirty-five degrees west longitude. Once more, Alice confessed her anxiety about the possibility of sinking, and again, her husband reassured her that Captain Davidson and his ship would see them safely to port. What neither of them knew at the time was that the vessel had, in fact, struck an iceberg in the same region on the 12th of August, 1912, just four months after the Titanic sank nearby. The story was reported in *The Inter Ocean*, a Chicago newspaper, which described the damage as "not believed to have been serious."

Two days later, the couple stood by the rail, so Alice could take a photograph of a passing iceberg. The wind was so cold that day that she wore her winter coat under Jack's army issue greatcoat. Just as they were about to get in out of the wind, Jack pointed to a distant grey-blue lump off the bow.

"That's Belle Isle at the entrance to the straight," shouted Jack above the noise of the wind.

In 1910, the island had been the first land Jack had seen after leaving Britain and now, nine years later, it was Alice's first glimpse of The Dominion of Canada too.

The *Corsican* docked at Quebec City on the 18th of August beneath an overcast sky. The mid-morning air was cool, about fifty degrees Fahrenheit, as the passengers prepared to disembark. Alice, who loved maps and had a good grasp of geography, thought it curious that the city's air was so uninviting since it was somewhat south of her home in London. She wondered, as she stood before the immigration officer, what the weather was like in Russell Square.

A Red Cross welcoming committee greeted the war-brides once they had passed through immigration, assisting with each family's transportation to the railway station and any other needs they had. With their guidance, Jack sent a telegram to his father, providing details of their anticipated arrival in Hamilton.

The Colliers and the Harrisons boarded the west-bound train and chatted as Canada passed by the glass of the carriage's windows. With frequent stops at stations along their route, the journey to Hamilton's Grand Trunk Station took more than seventeen hours. They were met in Toronto by Jack's younger brother Sid and his wife Pearl. Together, they boarded the train for the final leg of their journey. The exhausted couple stepped onto the platform amid the excited greetings of Jack's mother and his eldest sister Connie, with whom Alice had gone to school years earlier.

The weary couple finally arrived at the Collier home well after midnight. The house was decorated with fluttering Union Jacks and a "Welcome Home" sign, but before they could lay their heads on a pillow, they were fed a meal that would rival a traditional Christmas Dinner.

Alice and Jack stayed with the Collier family at 572 Wentworth Street, North for a couple of weeks while they acquired a few essential household items and basic pieces of furniture. Alice's initial impression of Canada was not particularly flattering. One of the first things she did, after arriving in Hamilton, was to write a letter to her mum about her journey and about the city where she was destined to spend the rest of her life. With a population of slightly more than 100,000 souls, the industrial port city appeared rather small, unsophisticated and dirty. Hers was, after all, the perspective of a young woman who had grown up in the largest city in the world.

"Canadians aren't very friendly and the British who are living here are worse!" she wrote.

Though she made a conscious effort to hide her apprehension, Peter and Rosina sensed her disappointment.

CHAPTER SIXTEEN

THE DEPRESSION

Life in Canada was different for each of its immigrants. For fifteen-year-old Jack Collier, it had been a wonderful adventure in a strange land; not quite the "wild west" but still a land of pioneers at the time of his arrival. His triumphant return at the age of twenty-four was different. By then, Canada – at least the part with which he was familiar – had become home to him. He was comfortable with its customs and familiar with its geography. Alice's experience contrasted in almost every way. She had an intimate knowledge of London but almost no chance of ever seeing it again. She had a loving relationship with her parents, her brother, aunts, uncles, cousins and friends, none of whose voices she was likely to hear again in her lifetime. In Canada, everything was strange to her. She didn't know her way around, and the people appeared different and distant. Even among Jack's family, she felt like an outsider. In those first years, only her love for her husband, and her friendships with May Harrison and Jack's sister, Connie, sustained her.

161 Oak Avenue, Hamilton, Ontario, as it appeared a century after Alice and Jack lived there.

Shortly after their arrival in Hamilton, Alice and Jack rented two rooms on the upper floor of 161 Oak Avenue from Jack's younger brother, Sid, and his wife, Pearl. The ceilings were sloped and the rooms were claustrophobically small.

With their living expenses eating away at his final pay-out from the army, Alice's husband began a search for work. It was only natural that he sought employment as a glove cutter, but the Hamilton Glove Company was no longer in business, and the Imperial Glove Company had no positions available. He wrote to Frank Byford in Georgetown and learned that the Ontario Glove Company in Kitchener, Ontario was hiring.

Alice, who had been exposed to anti-German propaganda throughout the war, was unwilling to live in a town predominantly inhabited by German immigrants. In fact, the community had been known as Berlin until mid-way through the Great War. Then an odd coincidence occurred when, in response to growing anti-German sentiment, the town was re-named *on the very day that Jack sailed from Halifax to fight the German Army*. The name "Kitchener" was chosen to honour Field Marshal Lord Kitchener, a prominent British military figure.

Alice was adamant, but Jack needed an income and accepted a job with the Ontario Glove Company. He accommodated his wife's refusal to move to Kitchener by boarding near the gloveworks and commuting to Hamilton on weekends to visit his wife and daughter. The compromise made the young couple's life difficult, especially after Alice gave birth to her second child four days before Christmas. Their new-born daughter, Dorothy Pearl, conceived in England and born in Canada, was the first of four Canadian-born children. The baby was baptised at Hamilton's Church of St. Matthew, on Barton Street East near Oak Avenue on the 28th of March, 1920.

Trapped in two rented rooms, caring for two infants, and otherwise alone for five days out of every seven was not Alice's idea of marital bliss. Both she and Jack recognized within weeks that something would have to change, but tens of thousands of recently-returned troops were in a similar position. Jobs were hard to find, and the war-time demand for military supplies had come to an end, leaving industry with greatly reduced markets.

The government had accumulated a war debt well in excess of one-and-a-half billion dollars, and the economy was slipping into a post-war recession.

Jack had managed to save a little money during the war, and he received a war service gratuity and separation allowance when he was discharged. After returning to Canada, he spent cautiously and continued to add to his savings with the intention of buying a house some day. His skill as a glove cutter earned him a good wage, and he enjoyed the work and might have remained at Ontario Glove, but neither he nor Alice could tolerate his absence from home. In the spring of 1920, he bought a house just beyond Hamilton's eastern city limit. *Then*, he told Alice.

"I've bought us a house," Jack blurted with obvious pride.

"A house?" replied Alice, "What do you mean? Where? How could you buy a …"

"It's a nice little house in Homeside just outside the city. It was only $1,800 and I put down a deposit of $300.

Jack paused, but Alice was too stunned to say anything, so he continued, "The previous owner has agreed to give us a mortgage for $1500 at six-and-a-half per cent. Our payments won't be much more than we're already paying for rent, and it'll be our own."

Alice was so surprised, she could barely think. "Then, we'll be moving. When? When will we be moving?" she asked, "How many bedrooms are there?"

"Next Saturday," Jack answered.

"What, April 10th?" queried Alice.

"Yes, we'll pack up as soon as I get home Friday night. Joe and Sid are going to help us move," Jack explained, Sid's arranging a lorry to move our things.

Alice was shocked and felt like she had little control over what happened in her life, but she was delighted that she would soon be free of the confining rented rooms. Her sister-in-law had not been an ideal landlady, often complaining about the noise of Alice's footsteps and the baby's crying. She seemed preoccupied with the expense of her tenant's electricity. Pearl began turning off the power to the rented rooms on weekdays until she saw her husband coming home from work. It appeared to Alice that Sid wasn't aware of his wife's behaviour, but she didn't complain to him or Jack because she didn't want to cause trouble with her in-laws.

"Aren't you pleased to have a house all to ourselves?" asked Jack.

"Yes, of course Jack," conceded Alice, who was feeling a little conflicted about the unexpected move.

Alice had clung to the possibility that she might some day convince Jack to return to England and live there, close to everything she missed. The purchase of a house in Canada pushed that hope beyond reach.

"Why didn't you tell me, Jack?"

"I just heard about it, and I wanted to surprise you," responded her husband.

The following Saturday, Alice made breakfast, cleared up, and dressed the girls to go to their new home.

While automobiles were becoming commonplace on the city's streets, most were owned by the wealthy or small business owners. Rather than hire a moving company to relocate their few belongings, Alice's brothers-in-law, Sid and Joe, loaded them onto a borrowed lorry and made their way to Homeside while Alice and her family walked the short distance to Barton Street to board an eastbound electric streetcar. Rain had fallen through the night, and the atmosphere remained cold, damp and overcast.

When the Colliers arrived at the Kenilworth Avenue stop at the eastern boundary of the city, they stepped off the street car into sticky wet clay. Jack had twenty-month-old Connie in his arms, and Alice was carrying baby Dorothy when her shoe was suddenly sucked off her foot by the mud.

"Jack! Jack! My shoe! I've lost my shoe. Help me!" cried Alice as she stood on one foot, trying desperately to maintain her balance.

Jack came to her rescue immediately, but found it difficult to suppress his grin.

There were no sidewalks or streetlights in Homeside as it was still beyond the city limits; just unpaved, muddy roads and open fields between ragged clusters of houses.

"It's practically in the country," Alice noted.

Jack sensed her disappointment and said nothing in response.

Together, they walked eastward along Barton Street to Alexander Avenue and turned southward for a couple of blocks to Albany Street. When Jack pointed out the little house, Alice had mixed feelings. The structure was rather small, and it sat directly on the ground with no "cellar" beneath it. Its only redeeming features appeared to be a large covered veranda and a low white picket fence that surrounded the front yard. The damp air, grey sky and red clay mud did little to enhance the house's appeal. Alice was unimpressed, but she could see that Jack was proud of providing a home for his family, so she suppressed her concerns. Jack cringed when she learned that the house had no indoor plumbing, and they would have to get their water from a well around the corner. He quickly assured her that he would fix up the tiny cottage just the way she wanted it – *over time*.

84 Albany Street (later known as 128 Albany Avenue) as it appeared on 20 August 1920

When the neighbourhood was later incorporated into the City of Hamilton, Alexander Street became Harmony Avenue, and the Collier home was redesignated 128 Albany Avenue. Jack bought a number "one" and number "two" stamped out of tin to match the "eighty-four" already tacked to the wall beside the door. It saved him the expense of buying a new "eight."

Jack knew that once they moved into their new home, he would find it difficult to maintain the house while commuting to and from Kitchener, so he made a concerted effort to find work nearby. When his sister, Connie, who was employed by Meakins Brush Company in Hamilton, told him about a job there, he applied and got the position. It didn't pay as well as glove-cutting, but at least he would be able to come home from work at the end of every day to eat supper with his wife and children.

A short walk from Jack and Alice's new home, at Barton Street and Kenilworth Avenue, there was a race track known as The Jockey Club. It had opened the year before Jack was born and had become a well-known landmark in the city. Though he was in no position to pay the Jockey Club's entrance fee on race days, he occasionally participated in the working-class practice of squinting through the narrow gaps in the green-painted board fence that surrounded the track. Over time, he acquired an intimate knowledge of the widest gaps and largest knotholes through which he could watch a race or two.

In the summer of 1920, the Manson family emigrated from Glasgow, Scotland, and moved into 130 Albany Avenue, next door to Alice and Jack. Though their home towns and childhoods were dissimilar in many ways, Mrs Manson and Alice became friends and supported one another as they adjusted to life in Canada.

Alice missed her family terribly, particularly on special occasions like her birthday. She wrote to her mum regularly and listened anxiously for the postman in the hope of receiving a letter postmarked "London." When Jack came in from pottering in the garden on September 19, he found his wife crying and tried to comfort her.

"It's Mum's birthday today, she's forty-seven, and I miss her so much," cried Alice.

Jack knew the underlying cause of her unhappiness was her love for him. He felt responsible and yet helpless. He didn't know what to say, so he simply held her hand for a few minutes as she wept.

Alice lost weight over the next couple of years and struggled to find the strength to cope with her duties as a wife and mother.

Just three years earlier, Sigmund Freud had theorised that melancholia was a response to a perceived loss which manifested in unconscious anger and self-dissatisfaction. While he favoured psychoanalysis as a treatment, most doctors remained ignorant of his research and considered the condition an inherited brain disorder. Decades passed before the conditions now known as "depression" and "postpartum depression" gained common acceptance.

Alice took the medication that her doctor prescribed, but it seemed to have little, if any, effect. She gradually came to accept her separation from her loved ones in England though years passed before she was her cheerful self again.

Throughout their lives, the Colliers witnessed one innovation after another as capitalism nudged technology ever forward. On the Saturday following his last payday before Christmas, Jack took Alice uptown to shop for gifts, insisting they visit Robinson's department store because the retailer had just installed a moving staircase, and he wanted to try it out. Little Connie and Dorothy were too young to take notice and grew up taking such things as automobiles and escalators for granted.

The following summer, Sid Collier established a garage on Kenilworth Avenue where he repaired automobiles, sold and serviced batteries and operated a small store. While in that store a year later, Alice heard music emanating from "a machine" on a table. She had never seen a radio, and wasn't aware that almost forty stations were then broadcasting regular programming in Canada. Sid explained that the music she heard was coming from Buffalo, New York. Alice was amazed.

Some time afterward, Sid gave the radio to Jack as repayment of a debt. In the evenings after dinner, Alice sat before the cumbersome device, carefully adjusting the tuning knob in search of stations. She delighted in listening to broadcasts from New York City; Lincoln, Nebraska; Winnipeg, Manitoba; and other cities around the world. On one occasion, she heard a program from Tokyo, Japan, which included a request in English for distant listeners to write to the radio station. It was a practice employed by radio stations at the time to gauge the effectiveness of their transmissions. Alice enjoyed writing to broadcasters and collecting their acknowledgements which came in the form of special postcards bearing the stations' call signs. The postcard from Tokyo was her favourite, and one she cherished for decades.

In 1922 Jack went to work at Burrough, Stewart & Milne, a coal and wood stove manufacturer on Hamilton's Burris Street. The pay was slightly higher than it was at the brush factory, the work was more appealing, and he managed to allocate some of the extra income to renovating the house to make it a little more comfortable for his family.

Jack's friend, Bill Harrison, was working at the Canadian National Railway's Hamilton freight yard in 1923 and suggested Jack could earn better money there than at the stove factory. Always eager to improve his income, Jack secured a job there as a cargo porter and a labourer assigned to local track repair.

In late February, 1924, Alice received a letter from her mum advising that her father had recently improved his situation by acquiring the position of maître d' at London's Imperial Hotel. Rosina Geherty proudly enclosed a photo of him and the hotel's waiters along with a small promotional pamphlet describing the hotel's services and amenities.

Rear and front covers of Imperial Hotel promotional pamphlet detailing hotel services, amenities, and prices.

The prestigious facility boasted 1,000 rooms, "the finest Turkish baths in the world," and featured an orchestra which played daily in the hotel's sumptuous Winter Garden. The rooms were advertised as "fitted with running hot and cold water" as well as a "hot-water radiator." The price of a single room, including breakfast and boot cleaning, was ten shillings, sixpence. Alice wished she could go to London to see the hotel and perhaps walk through its lobby or peek into the dining room to watch as her father greeted the hotel's guests. Alice cherished the photograph and the pamphlet throughout her life, taking them out from time to time to look at them through tear-blurred eyes.

*Imperial Hotel, Russell Square, London;
Maître d' Peter Geherty in black tie (front row).*

After almost three years with the railway, Jack applied for a job at Hamilton's International Harvester plant, where his father was a timekeeper. In the employ of the company that claimed to be the *"largest agricultural implement works in the British Empire."* Jack's pay packet increased yet again. Alice was beginning to hope that through frugal spending she might one day return to England to visit her friends and family.

Alice's husband, like most of Canada's working class, had very little money to spend on entertainment. Still, she always had the housework done by the time Jack came home from work, and they found lots to do in the evenings and on weekends. Saturday evenings were often spent visiting with, or hosting, the Harrisons and playing cards. During hockey season, Jack and

Bill sat huddled around the radio, listening to the play-by-play broadcasts of the Saturday night games.

One of the Colliers' favourite places to go in the city was Gage Park, a seventy-acre municipal park which opened in January of 1922. They could take the children there in a few minutes by following the "pipeline," to Ottawa Street. From there, paved sidewalks made pushing the pram relatively easy. The water pipeline, built in 1859 in response to a cholera outbreak fifteen years earlier, provided a diagonal route through the otherwise built-up east end of the city.

One of their walks to the park in late June of 1925 had a specific purpose for Jack, who never acquired a driver's licence. He wanted to see the recently installed electric traffic light at the intersection of King Street and Main Street, a junction at the north-east corner of the park locally known as "the Delta." It was the very first electric traffic control in Canada, and he had read about its installation in the newspaper a few days earlier.

Sometimes, on hot summer Sundays, the Colliers made a journey to the beach or the amusement park at the Burlington Canal. Alice packed a lunch, and Jack carried it along with a blanket to spread out on the sand. Bathers came from all over the area to enjoy the beaches along the sand bar that linked East Hamilton to Burlington at the west end of Lake Ontario. Both of the girls were usually asleep long before the Colliers arrived home in the evening. After tucking them into their beds, Alice and her husband would recall their day over a cup of tea before they too went to bed exhausted.

On school days, Alice kissed her daughters goodbye, climbed the stairs to the back bedroom and stood at the window to watch them walk to school. Then she would set about cleaning, doing laundry, or perhaps walk to Kenilworth Avenue to shop for groceries. She bought fresh bread from Summerfield's Bakery, meat from Mr Lickman, the local butcher, and produce at the fruit market where Britannia Avenue crossed. The merchants were friendly and always found time to chat with each customer for a few moments. Alice appreciated that. With Jack at work, and so many of her friends and extended family members a continent away, she enjoyed the social interaction that went along with shopping.

Once again, in 1927, Jack found his wife upset about being so far from her family. She was sitting at the kitchen table with a letter in her hand and tears streaming down her cheeks.

"Grandma died," she said as he handed the letter to her husband, then sat quietly while Jack read it. Susan Smith, her maternal grandmother, was already in her grave by the time Alice received the letter. It was another cold reminder of what she had given up for the love of her man.

Jack joined the East Hamilton Great War Veterans' Association shortly after his return from Europe. By 1927 it had amalgamated with other veterans' groups to form Branch 58 of the Canadian Legion. Three years later, the City of Hamilton granted it a building lot at Barton and Agnes Streets, where the first club rooms were built. Jack was a founding member of the Branch 58 Colour Party and proudly carried the Union Jack in ceremonies and parades until his eventual death in 1985.

Alice never tired of reading about her changing world in the daily newspaper. In 1929, the *Hamilton Spectator* reported that the city's first "skyscraper," the 210-foot-high Pigott Building was nearing completion. The construction of the eighteen-storey structure, at the intersection of Main and James Streets, cost $1,000,000.

"Jack," suggested Alice, "Let's go uptown on Saturday to see the new Pigott Building and do some shopping. We could go to the farmer's market, Stanley Mills Department Store, and the Right House."

"All right dear," conceded Jack.

He would have rather spent the afternoon playing cribbage with his fellow veterans at the Legion, but his wife was pregnant, and he understood her need to get out of the house and away from her responsibilities occasionally. Besides, he was curious to see the new skyscraper too.

At the age of thirty-one, Alice gave birth to a third daughter on the 9th of August, 1929. The baby was named Myrtle Joan though she soon became "Joan" to everyone. Connie and Dorothy, who were then nine and eleven years old, enjoyed helping their mother look after their little sister.

The growing family in the little house on Albany Avenue was content. Giggles emanated from the girls' bedroom for a while after bedtime almost every night. Jack had what appeared to be a secure, well-paid job, and Alice had regained the beautiful smile that had first attracted the machine-gunner in the summer of 1916.

Both Alice and Jack read the daily newspaper thoroughly, and while they had an elementary understanding of economics, they didn't fully appreciate the complexities of the financial world and national economies. When the stock market crashed suddenly on the 29th of October, the Colliers were concerned, but they didn't initially comprehend the impact it would have on their lives and those of their friends and neighbours.

> October 29, 1929 marked the beginning of the Great Depression, when more than 16 million stocks traded in the United States as shareholders scrambled to extract their money from the stock market. The day became known as "Black Tuesday" because the New York Stock Exchange lost fourteen billion dollars, and many of its investors lost everything they owned. The world fell into an economic collapse which severely impacted most people for much of the next decade.

Alice and Jack had been raised by working class parents and had struggled to make ends meet at times, but they knew nothing of what lay ahead. Stories of personal and corporate bankruptcy occupied column after column in the newspaper, and everyone was talking about closures and cutbacks. By the spring of 1930, slumping farm machinery sales began affecting International Harvester's production, and Jack started to worry about being laid off.

One of the benefits of working for International Harvester in 1930 was that the company offered financial assistance to its staff in the form of loans. Jack, who didn't believe in non-essential credit, had no intention of utilizing the corporate benefit, at least, not until one of his fellow workers pointed out that the first men recalled to work would be those who owed the company money. While he had no need of a loan at the time, Jack borrowed $500 and deposited it in his bank account just in case of a layoff. Then in August, he found himself out of work. Suddenly, the economic disaster of *The Great Depression* became a reality for Jack and his family.

By midway through 1933, farm machinery sales were down by 90 per cent, and thirty per cent of Canada's workers were without work.

CHAPTER SEVENTEEN

SECOND WIND

Alice gave birth to her fourth daughter, Shirley Virginia, on the 12th of September, 1930. Jack, having lost his job a few weeks earlier, had begun helping out at his brother's garage at 52 Kenilworth Avenue North. There wasn't enough work to warrant a full-time position, and Sid couldn't afford to pay very much, but it helped provide for the family while he looked elsewhere for employment. It had been almost a year since the stock market crashed, and a commonly heard claim in the neighbourhood was that jobs were "as scarce as hens' teeth."

A month or so after her husband began working at the Kenilworth Garage, Alice's eleven-year-old daughter, Dorothy, fell beneath the front wheel of the baker's delivery wagon. It was obvious to her mother that her leg was broken, but Alice had a new-born baby to care for and no telephone to summon Dr Guyatt. She made Dorothy as comfortable as possible on the girls' little red wagon and told Connie to take her sister to her dad at their uncle Sid's garage.

"Connie, please go slowly," pleaded Alice, "and do try to avoid the bumps."

Alice knew Sid's business had a telephone, and Jack would be able to call the doctor from there. Dorothy returned home several hours later, sporting a brilliant white plaster cast and immediately became a celebrity of sorts among the neighbourhood children.

The Great Depression was difficult for most of the working class, but it couldn't have come at a worse time for Alice who had, only recently, recovered from years of depression. Throughout the next four years, she had little or no money with which to provide clothes and prepare meals for her husband and her daughters. She found a multitude of ways to stretch what little Jack earned and made use of everything that was left over. She made the children's clothes, mended them as needed, and patched them when she couldn't buy material to replace them. She even made dresses for the little ones from cotton flour and sugar bags. She began by bleaching them to remove the brand imprint, then dyed the cotton before pinning the patterns to it and cutting out the pieces. She served the least expensive foods, like cabbage, spinach, peas, beans and potatoes, and the cheapest cuts of meat, especially liver and pork. She canned vegetables and fruits from the garden, made jam from raspberries and blackcurrants that grew there, and always seemed to find a way to "make do."

Above all, *Alice* went without.

Jack's wife was proud of him, even when he was unemployed. He was always a willing and diligent worker, and he never passed up an opportunity to earn a dollar. When, in 1931, Ontario's tobacco crop was ready to be harvested, Jack journeyed thirty miles to Hagersville to work as a picker. He camped near the tobacco fields so he would be available for work at sunrise, before the rest of the pickers arrived. Then he picked tobacco beneath the hot sun until it set, sending his fifty-cent-a-day earnings home to his family each week.

Jack tramped all over Ontario, selling Royal Canadian Legion calendars door to door, and participated in a city work programme known as *Man-a-Bloc*, wherein the residents of each city block were referred to a designated handyman in their neighbourhood. It didn't generate much work, but it helped him earn a little from time to time when nothing else was available. When he had no work at all, he spent his day looking for it. In addition to the fruit trees, berry bushes and vegetables he grew in the garden to help make ends meet, he kept a few chickens to supply his family with eggs. When he had no money to buy his daughters' birthday presents, he made them. Among the girls' favourite gifts were the doll houses that he built secretly in the basement.

On at least one occasion, Alice sent Jack and his eldest daughters to Gage Park to pick fruit for the park's grounds keeper. The park had previously been farmland and incorporated an orchard of apple and pear trees. The pickers were allowed to keep half of what they harvested as payment for their labour. Decades afterward, Jack's daughter confessed that her father hid a couple of baskets of fruit on the far side of the fence that day, to be collected on their way home.

Alice loved books and had been an avid reader since childhood. Reading was perhaps her favourite pastime though she spent hours knitting as well. Both activities became especially important to her during hard times, when other forms of entertainment were simply too expensive. She kept abreast of events throughout the world by reading the daily newspapers and weekly magazines. *The Saturday Evening Post* and *Life* magazines often passed the time while Alice drank a second cup of tea after Jack had gone to work. She was delighted when, in 1932, a branch of the city's public library opened just six blocks away on Kenilworth Avenue. It meant that no matter how little money she had, she could walk to the library, select an assortment of books, and bring them home to read at her leisure. After the children had gone to bed, she and Jack often sat quietly reading in the parlour together.

Jack endured four years of intermittent employment during The Depression. According to the city directory, he worked as a glass-cutter for a while in 1933, but many of his employment details for that period are rather vague. Early the following year, he worked as a handyman at Hamilton's east end crèche on Barton Street, a short walk from Albany Avenue. Finally, in the spring of 1934, Jack was recalled to his job at International Harvester where he worked continuously for the next five years. Within a few days of his return to work, he repaid the unspent $500 that he had borrowed from the company to ensure his recall.

After years of frugal spending and going without, Alice sweet-talked Jack into taking her uptown to the Pantages Theatre to see a movie. Connie, who was then sixteen years old, looked after her sisters while her parents went out for the evening. They walked to Main Street, rode the streetcar to the theatre on King Street East, and found seats in the centre of the balcony. The feature movie was *It Happened One Night*, starring Clark Gable and Claudette Colbert. The following year, the Kenilworth Theatre opened on the west side of Kenilworth Avenue just a couple of doors from Albany, and a Collier family tradition began.

On Friday nights, Jack, Alice, and the girls dressed for their weekly "night out" and walked together to Kenilworth Avenue. Theatres didn't have concession counters in the 1930s, so the family's first stop was the candy store next door. Once everyone had selected and paid for their sweets, Jack bought their tickets at the theatre box office, and they entered the Kenilworth's lavishly decorated lobby. Usherettes, armed with flashlights, waited at the theatre entrances to lead the patrons down darkened aisles to vacant seats. Then, they settled in to await the moment when the heavy velvet curtains parted to expose a projected image on a white, twelve-foot-high screen. Most often it was the MGM lion's roar that announced the movie's beginning. In addition to two featured films, the patrons were treated to a cartoon, a British Pathé Newsreel, and a short documentary. Often, after leaving the theatre, Alice and her family stopped in at a shop across the street to pick up fish and chips for an additional treat.

To entice movie-goers to attend regularly, the Kenilworth Theatre promoted a series of "dish nights," offering complimentary pieces of dinner wear. Those who attended regularly were able to collect complete place settings. For decades afterward, Alice's cupboards contained W. S. George floral-patterned china acquired at the Kenilworth Theatre's dish nights.

For many families, television was still two decades away when, on May 6, 1937, the German airship *Hindenburg* caught fire while landing at Naval Air Station Lakehurst in New Jersey. Thirteen passengers, twenty-two members of the crew, and one of the air station's ground crew were killed. Alice read about the disaster in the newspaper, but it wasn't until she saw the five-minute-long Pathé newsreel at the Kenilworth Theatre that she fully understood the magnitude of the horror.

Alice celebrated her fortieth birthday on June 23, 1938. Jack and the girls sang *Happy Birthday,* and Alice blew out the candles on her cake.

"I can't believe how quickly time has passed," she mused. "We've lived in this house for eighteen years, Connie and Dorothy are grown, and Joan and Shirley are eight and nine years old."

Jack had made numerous renovations to the house over the years. He had taken out a $230 second mortgage in 1927 to lift the house and put a basement beneath it, so he could connect to the city sewage system. In doing so, he added steps to the raised veranda, constructed a staircase to the attic, and installed an indoor bathroom with a toilet and sink. Then he finished the attic to provide two additional bedrooms, and added a rear veranda as well. Eventually, he rigged up a makeshift shower over the drain in the "cellar," but it wasn't until years later that he finally installed a bathtub.

In February of 1939, Alice returned from an appointment with Dr Guyatt and confided to Jack that she was once again pregnant.

About three weeks later, Alice received the news that her beloved father had passed away at age seventy-nine. He died on the 5th of March – *her brother Arthur's birthday*. She was devastated. For years, she had clung to the hope that some day she would return to London to visit her parents. In an instant – *in the time it took to read the shocking news* – that long-held hope vanished. Knowing that he was responsible for separating her from her family, Jack was unable to find words to ease her grief.

Alice never felt close to Jack's family, and often stayed home while he and the children went to visit them. In the spring of 1939, her in-laws rented the house across the street. It meant that they would be close at hand when Alice went into labour. Though it was her fifth pregnancy, she still found it comforting to know that she wouldn't be alone when the baby came.

Alice read the daily newspaper assiduously, and experienced déjà vu when it reported heightened political tensions in Europe that summer. Journalists were predicting that war was likely, if not inevitable. She and Jack discussed the implications in low voices to avoid alarming the girls though Connie and Dorothy, then twenty-one and twenty respectively, began bringing the subject up independently. They too were beginning to take an interest in Germany's sword rattling as many of their male friends would likely enlist in the event of war.

Jack was patriotic, physically fit, experienced and ready to serve, but he was forty-four years of age and had five dependents, so the Canadian government deemed him ineligible for active service. The International Harvester Company began shifting its focus away from farm implements in the early summer of 1939 and began re-tooling in preparation for war. When it started letting workers go, Jack commenced yet another search for work.

A friend from the Legion told Jack, "I heard the provincial police are hiring veterans to guard government installations against sabotage."

The following day, Jack began making inquiries, and within a couple of weeks had secured a security-guard position with the O.P.P. His assignments included patrolling commercial docks in Hamilton's harbour and guarding local hydro-electric facilities.

To facilitate urgent "call outs" Jack was expected to be available by telephone, so he arranged to have one of the neighbourhood's first phones installed. Alice was excited to have the modern convenience, and didn't mind at all that neighbours came by to use it on occasion. It would be handy for calling Dr Guyatt when she went into labour too.

As the summer of 1939 waned, Alice grew more concerned with the *Hamilton Spectator*'s reports of events in Europe. Signs of war had been apparent to her for some time.

Germany had annexed Austria in March of 1938, and had then occupied Czechoslovakia's Sudetenland in October. Jewish businesses and homes in Germany were vandalized on the night of November 9th and 10th, an event which came to be known around the world as "Kristallnacht" – *the night of broken glass*. In May of 1939, Germany and Italy signed an alliance described as a "pact of steel." It was followed three months later by a German-Polish treaty. By mid-August, a program known as "Operation Pied Piper" was put into effect in England and Scotland. It involved the evacuation of school-age children from British cities thought to be at risk of being bombed. The children were to be relocated to rural areas and villages where they were billeted with other families for the duration of the war.

Then, on September 1st 1939, the Nazis invaded Poland. Two days later, Britain, France, Australia, and New Zealand declared war on Germany, but it wasn't until September 10th that Canada formally joined the fight. Three days later, Alice's only son, John Albert Edward, was born into a world of chaos. Jack loved his four girls, but he couldn't help being thrilled that Alice had finally presented him with a son. He could hardly contain his excitement.

Alice, now forty-one years old, was exhausted. She had endured a difficult pregnancy and delivery, lost her father, and was unable to attend his funeral in England. Then, she watched as the governments of the world began sacrificing another generation of young men. Her memories of the Great War were still vivid, and the thought of living through another war was sobering, but she was relieved that at least her military-aged children were girls.

Little Jackie, as he had been known to the family since his birth, became the focus of the family. Everyone wanted to hold him, push his pram, and show him off. Then tragically, on the seventh of February, 1940, Alice's only son died of pneumonia. Jackie was a week short of five months old. For the first time in her life, Alice saw her husband cry. He was devastated.

The baby was buried in Hamilton's Eastlawn Cemetery.

The Colliers' eldest daughter, Connie, was to be

Baby Jackie's modest headstone in Hamilton's Eastlawn Cemetery.

married in the spring, but the death of her baby brother caused her wedding to be postponed.

The tensions of war increased when, on June 10, 1940, Italy declared war on the Allies.

In July, Alice's daughter, Dorothy, began working at National Steel Car, a Hamilton railway car manufacturer that had converted their production to artillery shells. Dorothy was assigned to quality control because her slender hands enabled her to inspect the inside of each shell for imperfections. Alice and Connie contributed to the war effort too. Connie worked at Mercury Mills on Cumberland Avenue, where military uniforms and parachutes were manufactured. Alice went to work at Tuckett's Tobacco Company, earning thirty-six cents an hour packing cigarettes to be shipped to Canadian troops overseas.

The war impacted every aspect of life. Newspapers reported the conflict's progress in great detail, and the government hastened to rebuild its long-neglected army, navy and air force. In the midst of this flurry of war-time activity, Connie married on the third of August. As she and her groom, Joe, exchanged their marriage vows, Italian troops invaded the British territory of Somaliland from Ethiopia.

Less than three weeks later, on August 21, the Collier family registered as required by the War-Time National Registration Regulations.

The following day, Londoners dashed for air raid shelters as the Luftwaffe bombed outlying areas of the city for the first time. Eighteen thousand tons of high explosives fell onto London's streets and gardens during more than seventy air raids between then and mid-May of 1941. During that period, London endured the heaviest bombing of the war. Alice, who worried constantly about her mum and brother, searched The Spectator for details of the areas impacted by the raids and let out a sigh of relief each time she received a letter from home.

October 4, 1940 was a significant day for Alice though she likely didn't give it a thought at the time. On that day, she had lived in Canada twenty-one years, one month and sixteen days, precisely the same length of time that she had previously lived in England. Most of her values, perceptions and habits, however, were acquired in the first half of her life and persisted until her death, so that she never lost her London accent, nor her predominantly English values and perspective.

During the winter of 1941, Jack was patrolling the city's docks in the early morning hours amid a wind-driven snowfall. He was uncomfortably cold and a little surprised when a military officer approached him out of the darkness. The man demanded that Jack identify himself and then ordered him to relinquish his rifle for inspection. Jack knew that giving up his weapon to *anyone* while on guard duty was contrary to military regulations, and he refused to comply. The officer bristled with anger and grabbed at the rifle in an attempt to take it by force. Jack stepped back, jerking the gun from the officer's grasp, and inadvertently slammed the rifle's butt into the man's jaw. The officer staggered backward and unleashed a verbal reprimand, consisting primarily of obscenities, then disappeared into the night. Jack heard nothing further about the incident.

"He knew I wasn't permitted to give up my gun," chuckled Jack decades later, "and he likely would have charged me if I had."

While inspecting munitions at National Steel Car, Alice's daughter, Dorothy, met a young pipe-fitter who also worked there. He impressed her on several occasions by bringing her bouquets of flowers. It seemed to Dorothy rather extravagant until she learned that her suitor's father was a florist. The family owned greenhouses on Province Avenue and had a stall at the Hamilton Market. Since the value of unsold cut flowers declined rather rapidly, her beau enjoyed a ready supply of fresh blooms with which to impress young ladies.

Within six months of their initial meeting, the florist's son proposed and Dorothy accepted. On the third Saturday of July in 1941, Joan and Shirley preceded their sister down the aisle of St. Paul's United Church as her flower girls.

Alice's first two grandchildren were born the following year when both Connie and Dorothy gave birth to sons. They were the beginning of a somewhat large family which would, by 1967, provide Alice and Jack with fourteen grandchildren.

CHAPTER EIGHTEEN

ALICE'S HERO

On May 23, 1940, Canada's Minister of National Defence announced the establishment of the Veteran's Home Guard to protect military and government facilities from sabotage. A few months later, the Home Guard was reorganised into the Veterans' Guard of Canada, consisting of both reserve and active companies.

On the 13th of July, German internees and prisoners of war began trickling into Canada from the United Kingdom. Most were German nationals who were in Britain when the war began. They were viewed as a potential threat to British security though many had actually fled from Nazi Germany to seek refuge in Britain. The remainder were detained merchant seamen, members of captured U-boat crews, and downed pilots. The Canadian Provost Corps provided security at Canada's POW camps until May of 1941, when The Veterans' Guard of Canada assumed the responsibility.

Alice's role as a homemaker became a challenge once again, when in January of 1942, rationing was introduced to deter hoarding and black-market profiteering. Purchases of gasoline, which was essential to the war effort, and liquor, a black-market favourite, were severely restricted. Foods like meat, flour, eggs, and cheese were in short supply in Canada because they were exported to Great Britain, where the population was more than triple that of Canada, and the capacity for domestic production was limited. Tea, coffee, sugar and other imports to Canada were also rationed. Coupons were distributed to each household in response to completed application forms. To prevent the sale of coupons on the black market, only merchants were authorized to tear the coupons out of their customers' ration books. Alice watched over her ration coupons carefully since they were even harder to come by than money. She budgeted her use of rationed products and adjusted recipes to compensate for shortages.

Jack continued to guard Hamilton's harbour and hydro facilities throughout 1942 and 1943 as a member of a reserve company of the Veterans' Guard.

Then, on 24 January 1944, after four and a half years in the employ of the Ontario Provincial Police, he enlisted in the 35th Company of the Veterans' Guard of Canada. It was one of the Guard's thirty-seven full-time *active* companies. For a second time, Alice kissed her husband goodbye and waited at home while he went off to serve his country.

Jack was deployed to Camp 23 at Monteith, nine miles south of Iroquois Falls, Ontario. It was one of thirteen internment camps in the province and had received its first detainees on July 14, 1940 at the site of what had once been a small lumber camp. They had been marched five miles to their accommodations along a bush road from the Temiskaming and Northern Ontario Railway line because there were no public roads into the camp. By the time the POWs disembarked from the train, they had seen nothing but trees, rocks and bodies of water for twenty-four hours, so they had no concept of where they were. The signs along the railway tracks were deliberately covered, and to deter escape attempts, the guards were prohibited from making any reference to the camp's location. Three ten-foot-high barbed wire fences, spaced at ten-foot intervals, surrounded the camp.

Corporal John A. Collier's hat badge

Initially, the facility housed 1,800 detainees though eventually 4,000 men lived within the barbed wire for a time. Both the prisoners and the guards endured black flies and mosquitoes in summer, and bitter cold and deep snow in the winter. They lived in draughty wooden barracks heated with locally cut wood, ate in mess halls, and relieved themselves in outhouses. The camp had a hospital, a post office, a library, a recreation hall, an ice rink, and guard towers perpetually occupied by armed sentries. The backs of the internees' shirts and jackets bore large red discs resembling targets. The implication was obvious to all.

Monteith POW Camp No. 23 Barracks

Few prisoners of war entertained the idea of escape because the camps were deliberately isolated and remote, and besides, they ate well, were treated well, and had a great deal of personal freedom. The inmates spent much of their time engaged in crafts, hobbies, reading and team sports such as soccer and hockey. Orchestras were organized and theatrical groups performed for fellow-detainees and guards. Some prisoners made pets of orphaned and injured birds and animals. Many of them were released back into the wild once they were capable of surviving on their own. Notable pets at Camp 23 included a blue heron and a pair of bear cubs named Nellie and Suzi.

Monteith POW Camp No. 23 Guard Tower

Some prisoners spent their time gardening, drawing and painting, or just keeping fit through physical fitness regimens. Those with specialized skills or knowledge provided instruction to others in the form of lessons and lectures. The vast majority of the materials for their sports and other pastimes were scrounged or provided by charitable organizations and international aid groups such as the YMCA. Though some inmates at Monteith found work in the camp's kitchen or laundry service; in maintenance, construction or chopping firewood; others sought employment opportunities beyond the barbed wire. Because the war left Canada critically short of manpower, the government was receptive to the idea, and it approved the employment of POWs in commercial lumber camps and on area farms prior to Jack's arrival. As a result, his duties often took him beyond the camp perimeter, escorting prisoners to and from work details.

On one occasion, Jack and another guard accompanied a group of POWs to cut firewood along the T&NOR tracks. When it came time to return to camp for supper, he discovered two men were missing. He and his comrade took the rest of the POWs back to camp, filled their bellies, and returned to the rail line around 9:30 p.m. With the low, summer sun obscured by the forest, darkness was about to consume the last of the evening's light. As Jack had anticipated, the two hungry men were sitting on the tracks vigorously scratching their mosquito bites. It didn't take long for most escapees to realize how difficult and uncomfortable it would be to survive in the Canadian wilderness. Attempted escapes were rare and with one noted exception, unsuccessful.

By the time that Jack arrived at Monteith in late February of 1944, most of the prisoners were German and Italian military personnel. Each of them had been assigned a colour to signify their allegiance to Nazism. Hard-line Nazis were designated "black" while anti-Nazis were identified as "white." Those POWs whose affiliation was split or unclear were assigned the colour "Grey," Jack wrote to Alice, describing the camp and its occupants.

"Most of the prisoners are OK and don't give me any trouble," she read.

According to Jack, one of the POWs was rather proud of his skill at draughts and went about systematically playing every inmate and guard until he was the recognized draughts champion of the camp. He sought ought everyone who was new to the camp within days of their arrival, and it wasn't long before he approached Jack.

"I can play checkers okay," wrote Jack, "but I didn't expect to beat him. When I won, all the boys whooped and cheered. Klaus was upset and wanted me to play again." Perhaps the champion had been overconfident and made a careless mistake, or was Jack simply lucky that day? In either case, he was just surprised as his opponent. The POW demanded an immediate re-match, but Jack refused the man's invitation. He took great delight in defeating the camp's "past champion" and never *did* give the poor man a chance to redeem himself.

> Franz Baron von Werra, a captured Luftwaffe pilot, was one of eight POWs who jumped from the window of a northbound prison train, shortly after it left Montreal in January of 1941. While the others were soon recaptured, Franz became the only POW to escape from Canada by crossing the frozen St. Lawrence River to Ogdensburg, New York prior to the US entering the war. Eventually, with the help of the German Consulate, he found his way back to Germany only to die nine months later on the 25th of October when his plane crashed into the North Sea on a training flight.

Railways were the life-blood of transportation in those days. In late June, Jack was granted a fourteen-day furlough and lugged his duffle bag from the camp to the rail line to catch a southbound train. It was late in the evening by the time he climbed the steps of the little house on Albany Avenue. Alice had let the girls stay up to greet their father, but she soon sent them up to bed, so she could sit with Jack over a cup of tea and listen to his stories about life at Camp 23.

From Alice's perspective, Jack's leave seemed to fly by, and before she knew it, she had kissed him goodbye and he was gone again.

With daughters Connie and Doris married, and her husband away in Monteith, forty-six-year-old Alice was alone with Joan and Shirley, then fifteen and thirteen respectively. She had faced considerable adversity in her life and felt capable of dealing with whatever came along, and yet, when she turned out the last light at bedtime, she felt vulnerable.

In the early morning hours of the 5th of September 1944, Alice was sleeping soundly beneath a crisp white sheet and a woollen blanket. The sash of the window beside the bed was propped up a little to admit fresh air, and the girls were asleep in the back bedroom upstairs. Night noises trickled in through the open window unnoticed.

At 12:38 a.m. Alice's bed began to shake and bounce about. Certain in that first instant that someone had jumped onto her bed, she awakened with a start.

Something crashed onto the floor in the kitchen and shattered.

Shirley called out in the dark, "Mommy! What was that?" Alice turned on the bedside lamp and flung her legs out from under the warm woollen blanket. Without being conscious of the act, she slid her feet into the slippers at the side of the bed. Her first thought was that something nearby had exploded. Canada was, after all, in the midst of a war. Long forgotten images of zeppelins and burning buildings flashed through her thoughts. She hurried upstairs to reassure the girls and look out the front-room window for an explanation. With Shirley and Joan close behind her, she opened the north-facing window and leaned out into the night, searching beyond the rows of houses toward the harbour for signs of a fire. Lights shone from the windows of several houses in the neighbourhood and a man was standing on the porch of a house across the street. Someone's front door slammed in the darkness to her right. Alice told the girls to go back to bed. Then she went downstairs, put on the kettle, and turned on the "wireless." While it warmed up, she swept the remains of a broken tea cup into the dustpan and dumped them into the trash can in the garden. Most radio stations had gone off the air at eleven or twelve o'clock, but Alice was determined and searched through the frequencies until she stumbled on an Albany, New York broadcast in the midst of reporting early details of the event. Amid a background of static and white noise, she heard the word, "earthquake."

The 5.8 magnitude tremor had been centred near Cornwall, an Ontario town on the northern shore of the St. Lawrence River. Days later, the estimate of property damage in the area stood at more than $2,000,000. What came to be known as the Cornwall-Massena Earthquake had reached 310 miles westward into the heart of Hamilton in an instant. There, it toppled the pinnacle of the eighteen-storey high spire of St. Paul's Presbyterian Church on James Street South. For years afterward, the fallen summit of the spire stood on the ground beside the church, a monument to the 1944 earthquake. Finally, in late 1989, a thorough restoration of the church included the pinnacle's return to its rightful place atop the steeple.

On the 11th of December 1944, Connie provided Alice with a fourth grandchild. Then it began to snow. By mid-day on the 12th, the city came to a standstill beneath more than two feet of blowing snow. Gale-force winds piled it up in doorways, alleys and intersections. Drifts grew to more than nine feet high.

An American Romance, starring Brian Donlevy and Ann Richards, was playing at the Capitol Theatre, but the film stayed in the can that day, and the theatre's seats remained empty for almost a week. With great determi-

> In pre-war Canada, postal workers sorted inter-city mail in mail-cars while trains carried it from town to town, so delivery was efficient and quick. In 1942, as a consequence of World War Two and the subsequent shortage of letter carriers, twice-daily residential mail delivery was reduced to a single delivery per day. In late 1945, with the discharge of military personnel underway, twice-a-day delivery was gradually resumed.

nation, most newspaper boys and mailmen succeeded in reaching their customers, but milk and bread delivery wagons were unable to navigate the snow-bound city streets. Late on the 13th, they managed to deliver their goods to designated pick-up locations around the city. Alice sent Joan and Shirley on a ten-block, round-trip expedition to a gas station on Britannia Avenue, to bring essential dairy products and fresh bread home on their sleigh.

The mailman's footstep on the veranda had always been significant to Alice. As a teenager in pre-telephone London, she had depended on the Royal Mail to communicate with her friends. Then, when the man she loved was living among the trenches on the continent, it was the mailman's approach that regularly caused her heart to skip a beat. Exiled from England, and missing her childhood home, the mailman became her tenuous link to her mum and dad. Finally, when Jack dressed in khaki for the second time and left for Monteith, his letters took the place of his cherished hugs and goodnight kisses. Throughout his deployment, the Canadian Pacific and T&NOR mail-cars carried hundreds of the couple's letters back and forth.

With "the storm of '44" and the excitement of Christmas behind her, Alice was in the kitchen clearing up the breakfast dishes on January 7, 1945. Though she didn't know it at the time, the day was about to become one that she would never forget. When she heard the postman on the veranda, she wiped her hands on her apron and hurried to retrieve the mail. She was hoping for a letter from Jack and perhaps one from her mother who hadn't written her in several days. Instead, she pulled an electric bill from the mailbox along with a manila envelope bearing a blue Canadian Pacific emblem and the word *"Telegram."*

Alice's trembling hands tore the envelope open as the wooden storm-door slammed behind her. The telegram read, "REGRET YOUR MOTHER PASSED AWAY SUDDENLY WEDNESDAY WRITING[.] ADA"

Alice barely managed to walk the short distance to the kitchen where she slumped onto a chair. She sat there for the better part of an hour before wiping away her tears and putting on the kettle to brew a pot of tea. Her next-door neighbour, Mrs Manson, came over and sat with her for most of the afternoon. Mrs Gibson, from across the street, brought over a macaroni casserole, so Alice wouldn't have to prepare a meal for the kids that night. After supper, Joan and Shirley cleared the table and washed and dried the dishes while Alice wrote a letter to Jack.

All traces of winter were gone when, in late March, Dorothy gave birth to Alice's fifth grandchild, another boy. While she and Jack's four surviving children were all girls, every one of their grandchildren up to that point were boys. In the end, only three of their fourteen grandchildren were girls.

Countless letters flew back and forth between Alice and Jack while they were apart. They shared the details of their separate lives with one another and looked forward to reading about each others' adventures. On the 23rd of April 1945, Alice wrote that she had obtained a prescription for new glasses and would be getting them in the next few days. The following day she wrote again, telling Jack that she and the children had influenza and assuring him that his parents were well.

On the twenty-fifth, Jack penned a letter to Alice.

"Here I am at 9:30 p.m.," he wrote, "sitting in a comfortable hotel room.

It's beautiful, has three beds, carpet on the floor, bed lamps, etc. I can see Spruce Falls on the Kapuskasing River through the window."

The hotel must have appeared somewhat luxurious to Jack who had spent the previous fourteen months in a remote POW camp.

"This is a beautiful inn," he continued, "and it's the prettiest place I've seen up north."

Jack was on escort duty with Captain Fogarty and a German POW doctor who was visiting prisoners at logging camps along the Kapuskasing River. He explained that they would be embarking early the following morning on a seventy-five-mile river trip.

Two days later, Jack wrote, "I'm at Camp 36 on the Kapuskasing River, about fifty miles from [the town of] Kapuskasing. I left Thursday aboard a motor cruiser called an alligator. The river is wide and dotted with floating logs. They're a constant danger, but the alligator is equipped with rollers and rides over them. I was squashed in the cabin with Captain Fogarty, the doctor, two girls who work in the Headquarters as waitresses, the pilot and four others. We towed a *pointer*, an open boat about twenty-five feet long – like a rowboat with a high pointed bow – loaded with two new canoes, mail bags, baggage and about six lumber-jacks. We went fifteen miles to Beaver Dock, arriving about 3:30 p.m."

Jack's letter went on to describe a portage around some impassable rapids that included a ride on a Spruce Falls Lumber Company rail line. They took the pointer with them, re-joined the river and arrived at Camp 15 in time for supper.

The group set out at first light the following morning with seven prisoners, three guards and fourteen others aboard. The pointer dodged logs and occasional cakes of ice as it fought its way upriver at about four miles per hour.

"We struck a log pretty hard and stripped the pin on the propeller shaft," wrote Jack. "but we repaired it and continued on. Then we hit another one just after 10 p.m. and bent the shaft, so we had to spend the night ashore around a blazing fire."

Alice read how the wind howled throughout the bitter night, and how her husband and his fellow travellers slept fitfully on spruce bows. Jack complained that they alternately "froze on the back and roasted on the front" and then "froze on the front and roasted on the back" in an attempt to keep warm. When the sun came up, they replaced the bent propeller shaft with a spare they carried in expectation of just such an occurrence. A mile up-river, they passed Camp 24, and though it was deserted, there were huts there that were equipped with stoves. If they had known how close it was, they would have hiked to the camp and might have spent the night in relative comfort. Two miles farther up-river, the band of mariners landed. Jack and some of the others boarded a truck for a four-mile ride through the bush to Camp 36 while the pointer continued on to Camp 37. The corduroy road they followed was constructed of thousands of similarly sized logs laid side by side. Track-like planks, spaced to correspond with the width of the truck's wheels, were nailed to the logs.

At Camp 36, Jack had a wash, then a sandwich and a couple of cups of tea. He remained near the stove to "get thawed out," and went to bed early.

Jack's third letter was written in his hotel room after returning to Kapuskasing: "The next evening, the doctor and I returned to the river via the corduroy road and continued on to Camp 37, twelve miles away and almost sixty miles from Kapuskasing. We had to stop at Camp 50 along the way, so we didn't arrive until 10:30 Saturday night – in complete darkness."

Jack remained at Camp 37 throughout Sunday. He had no duties for the day, so he found time to explore the area, rest, and play cards with the other guards at the camp. Before going to bed, he listened to a radio broadcast of the Charlie McCarthy Show, a popular comedy program of the 1940s. On Monday, he rose early, ate breakfast at 6 a.m. and began the return trip to Kapuskasing, arriving at the dock shortly after 5 p.m. He closed his letter with a description of the meal served at the inn that night.

"Pork chops, duchess style potatoes, spinach, pickles, bread & butter, baked apple, tea, and then apple pie," crowed Jack.

> World War Two's European hostilities ended on the 7th of May 1945, when in Berlin, Germany's Field Marshall Wilhelm Keitel signed an unconditional surrender of German Forces just prior to midnight. May 8th was declared "VE Day" (Victory in Europe) and people took to the streets to wave flags, cheer, sing and dance. Crowds surged through the streets of London, Paris and downtown Hamilton, Canada.

Four days after his return to camp, Germany surrendered.

The 35th Company was transferred to Camp 100 on the north shore of Lake Superior, and Jack's pay rate was increased by 10¢ to $1.50 per day. He liked the idea of being near the world's largest freshwater lake. In fact, his H-hut was just a few feet from the sandy beach. Both the prisoners and the guards enjoyed swimming in the lake occasionally, and Jack was able to go fishing when he was off duty. Still, the remote location of the camp meant a two-day trip to get home by train, and he wasn't looking forward to what was sure to be a much longer and colder winter than Alice and the girls would experience in southern Ontario.

Jack's responsibilities didn't cease when the European war ended on May 7 1945, nor did the August 15th announcement of Japan's surrender have any significant impact on his duties.

Thirty-four thousand German POWs waited anxiously within barbed wire enclosures for months while military bureaucrats made arrangements to send them home. The Canadian government had its hands full returning its own liberated POWs, a million other military personnel, and 70,000 dependent wives and children.

Alice and her husband were separated by more than 750 miles of railway track, most of which ran through forests, rock cuts and bushland. They might just as well have been at opposite ends of the world, so they cherished the few days they had together in the summer of 1945. Jack was granted fourteen days "privilege leave" in late August along with four days travel time, rations and allowances. He was glad to be home for the first time in a year and have the opportunity to meet his fourth and fifth grandsons for the first time. He was somewhat surprised how aware he had become of the city's noises. He found them much less appealing than the sounds of rustling leaves, breaking waves and the chirping of birds. By the end of his leave, he had become acclimatised to the city

Jack Collier and fellow Veterans' Guards aboard HMT Aquitania *in March 1946.*

and had again stopped noticing the urban cacophony of sound.

On his return to camp, Jack was advised that he had been promoted to lance corporal. He immediately began serving as an acting corporal and received the corresponding rate of pay.

In March of 1946, Jack's platoon, led by Lieutenant Rodgman, was assigned to escort 3,000 POWs to Halifax where they boarded Her Majesty's Transport, *Aquitania*. It was Jack's fourth Atlantic crossing, each time on a different ship and under very dissimilar circumstances, except that on three of those occasions he wore a Canadian military uniform. The *Aquitania* sailed on the 26th of the month, and the crossing was pleasant and uneventful. The ship was filled to capacity with amiable Germans, anxious to see their homes and loved ones. Jack, who hadn't been to London in twenty-seven years, was eager to revisit the city of his childhood. He was dismayed however, when having fulfilled his duties, he went there on leave.

Jack was appalled by the damage that the Luftwaffe's bombs had inflicted upon the capital. Toward the end of the month, Alice received a letter posted shortly after his arrival in London. He wrote in some detail about the "terrible destruction" throughout the war-ravaged city.

"Everywhere you go," he wrote, "you see heaps of bricks and rubble blocking the pavements."

Jack's visit to London wasn't entirely dispiriting. After his return to Canada, he sent his family a photograph of himself standing on the steps of the National Gallery of London. The gallery's art had been removed for safe keeping during the war, and Myra Hess, a renowned British pianist, had made regular concert appearances there throughout the war. Jack, along with other members of his platoon, had attended her final performance on the tenth of April.

On its return to Canada, the 35th Company was reassigned to Camp 10 at Fingal, southwest of St. Thomas, Ontario. It meant the end of the bitter-cold northern winters, and the warm weather hordes of blood sucking mosquitos and black flies. More importantly, it meant Jack would be able to go home to see his family occasionally. Alice was delighted.

The European war had been over for a year when Jack was confirmed to the rank of corporal. Alice had always been proud of her husband, especially the way he looked in his military uniform, but the two chevrons on his sleeve conveyed the army's approval of his performance and sweetened her pride.

Again, in late August of 1946, Jack was granted a fortnight's leave, but he wasn't able to get home for Christmas that year. He had embarked on his second escort duty to England on the 19th of November and didn't get back to Canada until January 21, 1947. His daughter, Connie, had given birth to his first granddaughter, Margaret Elizabeth, during his absence, and he was anxious to see her and hold her. She was two months old when they finally met for the first time.

On the 4th of March, 1947, after thirty-seven months of active service, Alice's hero was discharged from the Veterans' Guard of Canada at the age of fifty-two. While she had coped admirably with the upkeep of their house and garden, and managed the family's finances in his absence, she relished a break from the responsibilities and was glad to have him by her side again.

With the experiences of two wars now an integral part of his character, Jack returned to his family, but he never stopped being a soldier. As a member of the Royal Canadian Legion's Branch 58 Colour Party, he regularly polished his medals, donned his dress uniform, and marched through the streets of Ontario's towns in countless parades. He never missed a Remembrance Day Service, and on the 11th of November, 1984, at the age of ninety, Jack stood proudly in front of the Hamilton Cenotaph to take the salute on behalf of those who served in Canada's wars.

CHAPTER NINETEEN

THE GOOD YEARS

The post-war era marked the beginning of a new phase in Alice's life. Her daughters, the youngest of whom turned seventeen in 1946, were about to become independent, and she and Jack's long separations appeared to have come to an end. While they had struggled economically throughout their marriage, they never spent beyond their means, and both were satisfied to live a modest, working-class life. With her parents gone, the desire to "go home" was less appealing, and Alice looked to the future with contentment.

On January 2, 1948, Alice and Jack paid off the mortgage on their Albany Avenue home. Alice was pleased and proud that they no longer owed money to anyone. She tucked the discharge papers into a box along with some other important documents and put the box in a little cabinet in a corner of the bedroom.

When government military contracts dried up, manufacturers began reorganising their resources and technology to serve consumers. Signs of prosperity and innovation were everywhere. The manufacture of automobiles had been suspended during the war but it resumed in 1947 – and every returning soldier wanted one. Studebaker Canada established an assembly line in a Hamilton plant that had, until recently, built anti-aircraft guns. The first vehicle came off the assembly line on the 18th of August, 1948.

Neither Jack, Alice, nor any of their girls ever had a driver's licence, so the Collier family never owned a car. It was a little inconvenient at times, but they always managed to get where they needed to go. They walked to local destinations, and when the weather was inclement or the distance was too great to walk, Hamilton's electric streetcars provided a practical and affordable alternative. The city's railway stations offered passenger service to just about anywhere the Colliers might have to travel outside of Hamilton.

When Canada's first drive-in theatre opened on July 10, 1946, however, Alice was a little disappointed. The idea of watching a movie while sitting in a car sounded like fun, and the new drive-in was so close – just east of the city in nearby Stoney Creek – but she kept her disappointment to herself.

In 1949, when the recently constructed Gage Park band shell began offering Sunday concerts, Alice and Jack walked the intervening mile and a half to enjoy the open-air performances. It was a pleasant stroll, much of it along a grassy water-pipe-line right of way. Most often, they rode home on a streetcar, opening a window to allow the evening breeze to wash over them.

Not long after his discharge from the Veterans' Guard, Jack began working at Building Products Limited on Beach Road. Each morning, Alice wrapped his sandwiches in waxed paper, filled his thermos with steaming tea, and handed him his lunch pail as she kissed him goodbye at the door.

The 21st of November, 1948, began like any other day. Alice did some laundry and hung it on the clothesline to dry. After lunch, she began ironing. In mid-afternoon, while she was pressing one of Jack's shirts, the doorbell rang. When she opened it, a man in a suit introduced himself as a manager from Building Products Limited.

"Mrs Collier," he began, "there's been an accident."

Alice didn't remember much of what he said after that, but she recalled turning off the iron, grabbing her purse, and hurrying down the front steps to a car to be rushed to Hamilton's General Hospital. After an agonizing, seemingly endless wait, she was led into the hospital's burns ward. With his entire head, hands and parts of his upper body wrapped in white bandages, Jack was unrecognizable. Alice felt faint and held onto the bed's rails to steady herself.

Jack suffered severe burns to his face, neck and shoulders when molten asphalt splashed over his upper body, blocking his airways. Desperate for air, he clawed at the burning, viscous tar with his fingers and poked at it with his tongue, severely burning the tip of the latter. Unable to speak and heavily sedated, he lay perfectly still on his hospital bed.

Alice was terrified. Had her beloved Jack been taken from her forever? Someone brought her a chair and urged her to sit down. She couldn't tell if he was conscious or not, but she told him she was there, and sat with him throughout the evening. Much of the time, she cried softly.

Alice recalled sitting beside his bed at Bearwood Convalescent Hospital more than thirty years earlier.

"He survived that and he'll survive this," she said to herself, but her confidence was thin.

Within a couple of days, Alice was assured by the family doctor that Jack was going to recover.

"His recuperation will take several months." said Dr Guyatt, "but aside from the scars, he should make a full recovery."

The doctor explained that Jack would have to remain in the hospital, so his burns could be regularly treated to guard against infection. Alice and Jack faced yet another long separation.

Jack had proven to be a fighter throughout his life. By Christmas, he was well enough to paint the ward's windows with depictions of poinsettias, snowflakes, and holly. He even convinced Dr Guyatt to let him go home on Christmas Day for a short visit with his family. By then, because he was unable to shave his severely burned face, he had grown a full beard. His daughters feigned surprise, pretending to mistake him for Santa Claus. After a few hours with Alice and the girls, he returned to the hospital where he remained until the spring of 1949.

> 1948
>
> ## Blazing Asphalt Sprays Workman
>
> With blazing hot asphalt splashed over his face, head, and neck, John Collier, 120 Albany Street, was rushed to the General Hospital just after mid-day yesterday. Mr. Collier was working at Building Products Limited plant on the Beach Road when, it was reported, a plug flew out of a container and asphalt at a temperature of 350 degrees splashed out over him.
>
> At the hospital, it was reported that he had suffered second degree burns on his whole face, his ears, the left side of his neck, and his collarbones. The asphalt was still on Mr. Collier's face when he was taken into the emergency room at the hospital and it was cleaned off there. Authorities at the hospital described his condition as fair.

November 22, 1948
newspaper article

Jack filled his hospital days with reading, crossword and jigsaw puzzles, and playing cribbage with his fellow patients. Prior to the accident, he had acquired a set of moulds and had cast dozens of miniature lead soldiers in his Albany Avenue basement. His daughters, Joan and Shirley, had often sat on the cellar stairs watching as he poured the molten metal into the moulds. During his hospital recouperation, he eased the tedium by meticulously painting each figure in bright enamel colours. Over time, he gave sets of toy soldiers to several of his grandsons as gifts. They played with them for hours at a time, not knowing that "Papa" had painted them while he was recovering from his accident.

Jack continued making lead soldiers for several years. Some were sewn to cards which had been cut to fit tie boxes, and sold through Kenilworth Avenue's retail merchants in the days leading up to Christmas.

Jack recovered from his burns and returned to his job at Building Products. In 1951, he came home from work one day and handed his lunch pail to Alice, who was surprised to find it as heavy as it had been when she had given it to him in the morning. She was about to scold him for not eating what she had prepared when a black and white kitten emerged from the lunch box. Jack had seen the scrawny feline wandering about the plant property for days. It appeared to be homeless and constantly in search of something to eat. He had been feeding it bits of his lunch.

"What shall we call him?" queried Jack.

Alice, who had come to know Building Products Limited as *BP*, replied, "BeePee!" and the matter was settled.

BeePee became a beloved member of the Collier family throughout the 1950s.

One of Hamilton's largest employers in the 1950s was the Canadian Westinghouse Company. In 1948, it designed and manufactured the first Canadian-made television. Over the next five years, a small number of television antennas began to appear on roofs throughout the city. Initially, they were rare curiosities and somewhat prominent indicators of a family's prosperity. In the spring of 1953, Alice was invited by Mrs Gibson, a neighbour who lived at number 131, across the street, to see her brand new "TV." It was the talk of the neighbourhood.

Mrs Gibson's TV had been purchased in anticipation of an upcoming event. On the morning of the 2nd of June, her living room was filled with friends and neighbours who had been invited to watch the coronation of Queen Elizabeth on the TV's diminutive screen. Favoured guests came early and were offered seats on the sofa and lounge chair in the parlour. Kitchen chairs were brought into the room to accommodate those who arrived later. Still others sat on the floor or stood leaning against the walls. The neighbourhood children, including some of Alice's grandchildren, crowded around the open living room window and watched the snowy, black and white ceremony from the veranda.

Alice and Jack infrequently consumed alcoholic beverages. Their preferred cold drink was ginger ale, and they always had a case of twelve 26-ounce bottles in the basement as well as one in the ice-box. A Diamond Beverages truck picked up the empties and dropped off a full case every month. Visiting grandchildren came to anticipate a bubbly glass of the pale yellow liquid almost as soon as they arrived, in response to their transparent declarations of, "Nanna, I'm thirsty."

In September 1953, Alice watched as Jack walked his daughter Joan down the aisle of Ryerson United Church, kissed her cheek, and gave her away to her groom. They returned home after the reception with the last of their four girls, Shirley, who was that very day celebrating her twenty-third birthday. Her own wedding, twenty-six months later, marked the beginning of yet another distinct period of Alice and Jack's relationship. For the first time in their lives, after more than thirty-six years of marriage, they had one another all to themselves.

An explosion of post-war technology was changing the lives of the working class. In 1954, Alice explained to Mr Pickering, the man who had delivered ice to her three times a week for years, that her husband, Jack, had bought her a Leonard electric refrigerator. No longer would she put the ice card in her window to indicate to him what size of ice-block she required. No longer would Jack spill melt-water onto the kitchen floor as he carried the drip pan to the back door to dump it onto the garden. Though she looked forward to the convenience of the shiny, white appliance, Alice was a little sad that she wouldn't be seeing Mr Pickering anymore. Many of her social interactions were related to home deliveries of one sort or another.

By the end of 1956, the Colliers had two more grandchildren, a modern chrome dinette suite, and their very own television. The Motorola TV had an enormous twenty-one-inch screen, and the newborn babies were both boys. Alice was happy. She felt that life was treating her rather well, and the future looked bright.

Alice and Jack accompanied their daughter, Dorothy, and her husband on summer vacations to rented cottages in the 1950s. Their first week-long holiday was at Lake Dalrymple, a small hour-glass shaped body of water east of Orillia, Ontario. Jack and his son-in-law spent their days fishing while Alice and Dorothy enjoyed the summer sun and played with Dorothy's boys on the sandy beach. After a second holiday at Dalrymple the following year, they rented cottages on the shore of Lake Muskoka near Gravenhurst.

In 1955, Jack's employer, Building Products Limited, shut the Hamilton plant down in mid- summer for major renovations, so when their son-in-law's one-week holiday ended, Alice and Jack stayed on. Dorothy's boys stayed with their grandparents, and though her responsibilities were even greater than if she had been at home, the next few weeks became one of Alice's favourite vacations. In fact, it became an unforgettable summer holiday for all four of them. Most mornings, Jack and his grandsons loaded their lunch, fishing gear and bait into an open cedar strip boat right after breakfast. Then, pushed along by a five-horsepower Johnson outboard, they set off to one of Jack's favourite fishing spots. He liked nothing better than skewering a worm with a barbed hook and dropping it into the water to await the subtle tug of a small-mouth bass. Sometimes, after a lengthy wait, Jack would succumb to his tobacco addiction. He had a number of briar pipes, one of which was always tucked into his pocket along with a leather pouch containing his favourite tobacco. Inevitably, an unseen perch or sunfish would nibble on Jack's worm the minute he set his rod down to stuff his pipe with tobacco. He and his adolescent crew generally returned with ample perch and bass for supper. They scaled and gutted their prey at the end of the dock, feeding the heads and tails to the gulls as they worked. More often than not, Alice greeted them with a mild scolding for returning so late in the day.

It never occurred to Jack that Alice might be worried about someone drowning while they were out on the lake somewhere.

Once the dishes were washed and dried, the family gathered around the kitchen table and played rummy late into the evening. The chirps of crickets and the croaks of frogs enveloped the cottage in a boisterous chorus of night-sounds. Since air-conditioning had not yet made its appearance in middle class homes, open screened windows invited summer breezes day and night. Only on the chilliest of mornings, did Jack slip out from beneath the blanket in the pre-dawn light to close them until the morning sun warmed the outside air. When it did, Alice lit the fire in the woodstove, and the smell of sizzling bacon filled the cottage.

A cottage near the mouth of the Sauble River, where it empties into Lake Huron, and another on the southern shore of Lake Nipissing provided Alice with additional holiday memories in the 1950s. They were all pleasant escapes from the city's summer heat and noise, and Alice enjoyed spending the time with her daughter's family.

In 1958, Alice celebrated her sixtieth birthday and her fortieth wedding anniversary. The following year, Jack turned sixty-five and retired from Building Products Limited. He had an insatiable appetite for work and sought out part-time jobs, taking on small construction projects and gardening tasks for neighbours and friends at the Legion, cutting lawns and trimming trees and hedges throughout the summer. In the winter, he shovelled the snow from his sidewalks and then shovelled those of his neighbours, simply because he found inactivity intolerable. Besides, he, like Alice, enjoyed doing for and giving to others.

Jack spent more time at the Legion in the 1950s. He was always among the last to leave the hall after an event, having stayed to clear the tables, sweep up, and stack the chairs and tables. As an eager volunteer, a veteran of both wars, a member of the colour party and the cribbage league, he became well-known and popular among the members.

Jack studied the horses and occasionally spent an afternoon at the Jockey Club, conservatively betting his hunches. Alice indulged herself by playing bingo at the Legion and later at Holy Family Church hall on Tuesday evenings. Both of them enjoyed the prospect of winning though neither had forgotten the hard times, so they were unwilling to risk much. Jack's big win was a $36 daily double, and Alice eventually won full-card jackpot of $50 in the 1960s. Throughout the 1940s, and well into the 1950s, they bought tickets on the Irish Hospital Sweepstakes, the importation and selling of which was illegal in Canada. The ticket stubs were returned to Ireland where, three times a year, an official draw was held. The winning tickets were paired with horses running in featured annual races, and the ticket-holders' winnings varied according to the order in which the horses ran. Alice and Jack knew the odds of winning *any* prize were miniscule, but the act of buying a ticket gave them a moment of hope, often when some little luxury was just beyond their budget.

Early twentieth-century England, and its capital city London in particular, had subtly shaped and polished Alice in intangible ways that were blatantly obvious to those who knew her as an adult. Her friends and family recognized her as a Londoner, proud of her English heritage, her family and her sovereign. She kept an open mind, believing that every story has at least two perspectives, and rarely spoke a harsh word about anyone. In fact, she lived by the expression, "If you can't say anything nice about someone, don't say anything at all."

Alice had an abundance of love, encouragement and advice to share with those who were in need of it, and she was quick to recognize people's accomplishments, even when others deemed them trivial. She noticed details and learned lessons from them. Once, when one of her grandsons was about to leave the house for a job interview, she subtly reminded him of the importance of details.

"I can always always tell if a man is thorough by whether or not he's polished the heels of his shoes," she explained.

Thereafter, every time her grandson polished his shoes, he thought about her comment and resolved to be thorough in everything he undertook.

Alice passed her knowledge on to her descendants, sometimes deliberately and sometimes without being consciously aware of the gift she was giving. She taught her girls to cook and properly maintain a home. She taught them to sew, to knit and crochet, and through example, she taught them tolerance, understanding and empathy. When a family member lost his job, she responded with, "Everything happens for a reason."

"Don't worry, dear, something better will come along," she promised, and it always did.

Alice was invariably supportive of her family and friends, and contributed enormously to their successes – and subsequently, *to the world*. Her values became their values, and her quiet strength gave them strength as they faced adversity throughout *their* lives. She gently influenced others and changed the world in countless miniscule ways over many years.

CHAPTER TWENTY

ASHES TO ASHES

Branch 58 of the Royal Canadian Legion organized an affordable European tour on behalf of its members, their families, and friends. Jack came home from a meeting with the news in 1963 and had barely begun telling Alice about it when she blurted, "Oh yes, let's sign up!"

For Alice, it was a bittersweet moment when, after forty-four years of self-imposed exile, she had her first opportunity to return to England. With both of her parents deceased and much of the London that she remembered destroyed by the Second World War, she couldn't escape the sense of loss that haunted her. Throughout the war, newspaper accounts, along with her mother's letters, had detailed a long list of London landmarks destroyed during air raids. Still, seeing her brother, her friend, Nellie Marks, and some of her favourite places was for her an exciting prospect.

With the last of their daughters, Shirley, married in late 1955, Alice and Jack had managed to save a little, and immediately began planning for the midsummer adventure. Their long-time friends, Bill and May Harrison, and both of Jack's sisters joined the tour, along with many others they knew from the Legion.

Alice could not remember being more excited when she boarded the airplane. It was her first time flying, but she was more enthusiastic than anxious. She and Jack flew out of Toronto's Malton Airport aboard flight 570 at 9 p.m. on the 16th of July 1963. Alice kept a detailed journal of the flight, noting the precise times that the plane passed over Ottawa, Montreal, Quebec City and Newfoundland. She described the meals, the sunset, the sunrise, and the "clouds which looked like snowfields."

The Colliers settled into the Avalon Hotel, in Bloomsbury, very close to where they had lived on Coram Street in 1919. The following day, Alice and her brother, Arthur, were reunited after more than four decades of separation. Over the next week, the couple reacquainted themselves with other family members, friends, and their favourite places in London. Among the latter was Lyon's Corner House, near Charing Cross Station, Alice's once favourite place to eat. She took Jack there for dinner and later noted in her journal, "It cost us 15/ each – about $2.15."

Jack showed Alice where he had grown up on Trumpington Road and, where at the age of fifteen, he worked as a shop assistant after leaving Cann Hall Road School. Together, they visited Westminster Abbey, saw the new Waterloo Bridge and had lunch at Dirty Dick's. They spent nine days exploring London before taking the train to Newcastle to stay with Jack's brother, Sid, and his wife, Jean, for a couple of days. Sid had returned to England from Canada after his first marriage failed, and the brothers hadn't seen each other since. Alice looked on as the men talked about their shared past and exchanged stories about their separate lives. She understood what they were feeling as they became reacquainted after decades of separation.

Alice and Jack returned to London and immediately set out for Brighton where they spent a couple of days sightseeing and visiting one of Alice's cousins. On their return to London, they joined a Legion-sponsored tour to Belgium, Holland and France, where Jack delighted in revisiting the European towns and cities through which he had passed so long ago. Alice listened attentively as Jack reminisced about each of the places he recognized. Time after time, he looked about eagerly and provided a description of how a particular village had appeared in 1918. Then came a quiet pause, during which Jack was clearly staring into his past.

"What are you thinking about?" asked Alice.

"Nothing in particular," Jack lied.

It was August 16th by the time they unlocked the front door of 128 Albany. Jacked lugged their bags into the house and went downstairs to turn on the water. With a contentment she hadn't felt for decades, Alice filled the kettle and set about making a pot of tea.

Three months later, Alice and Jack sat in the parlour, watching the news coverage of John F. Kennedy's assassination. Alice was immediately reminded of the slaying of Archduke Franz Ferdinand in 1914. She had just turned sixteen when the story of his demise appeared in the *Daily Mirror*. At the time, she hadn't realized that she was witnessing the start of a war that would define her entire life. This time, as Walter Cronkite provided details about the US president's death, she understood that she was witnessing an historic event, and wondered what was yet to come.

Alice had lived through a great deal of hardship and turmoil, but she had overcome the challenges, and she was enjoying a more leisurely life as she entered her seventies. She was still reasonably healthy and active in many ways, but she was becoming less of a participant and more of a witness to history. She continued to read the newspaper every day and listen to the news on the radio, but the evening ritual of the eleven o'clock news on the TV added a new dimension to her understanding of world events. She *watched* Beatlemania sweep throughout the western world and *saw* the suffering of American soldiers in Vietnam. Then on the 20th of July 1969, along with an estimated 650 million people around the world, she and Jack watched Apollo 11 land on the moon and saw Neil Armstrong step onto its surface.

Jack, even healthier and more active than Alice, wasn't quite ready to assume the role of *spectator*. He continued to find part-time work and remained active in the Legion.

Jack was returning home from the legion late on a Friday night in 1966 when he observed a police officer escorting an inebriated rowdy out of the Kenilworth House, a local drinking establishment. As Jack approached, the man began struggling with the officer, and the pair tumbled onto the sidewalk in a frenzied heap. The assailant pinned the officer to the sidewalk and began assaulting him with his fists. Jack, then seventy-two years old, hauled the attacker off the officer and helped subdue the man. Then he went to the patrol car and radioed for assistance on the officer's behalf before continuing on his way home.

Throughout the 1960s, 1970s, and 1980s, Alice and Jack attended the weddings of their grandchildren and met the first of their great-grandchildren.

In April of 1975, Alice's brother, Arthur, passed away in England. With his death, another link in the chain that bound her to her past was severed.

In 1976, the Colliers flew to British Columbia to visit their daughter, Dorothy, who was then living and working in Vancouver. They took their great-granddaughter, ten-year-old Jacqueline, along to see her grandma.

Jack and Jacqueline held hands as they strolled through Stanley Park. They walked the beach at English Bay, picking up shells and colourful stones as the Pacific washed over their bare feet. Alice and Jack sat on a bench and watched as the sun set over the ocean. Jack even managed, one day, to go fishing while he was there.

Alice cherished her memories of that trip as did her great-granddaughter.

The following year, the aging couple celebrated their sixtieth wedding anniversary at a party arranged by their daughters. The local newspaper published a lengthy story about their enduring marriage, their British beginnings, and their immigration to Canada. For a short time, they were local celebrities and received congratulatory documents from their local member of parliament and the city's mayor. Five years later, on their sixty-fifth anniversary, similar congratulations came from the Prime Minister of Canada and Queen Elizabeth.

The devoted couple began slowing down in the 1980s, and became a little less active. Jack still pottered in the garden almost daily though he began spending more time relaxing in his recliner, smoking his pipe, and reading paperback novels. Zane Grey's Westerns were among his favourites. Perhaps it was Jack's enthusiasm for the Old West that attracted him to Grey's tales. As a boy, confined in a north-London classroom in the early 1900s, he had often daydreamed of becoming a cowboy in the American West. He also enjoyed Douglas Reeman's stories about the men of the Royal Navy in World War Two. Jack had sailed the North Atlantic seven times, and he could relate – *at least to some extent* – with the crews in Reeman's stories.

Alice's sight was failing, and reading was becoming a challenge. She had acquired a habit of holding the temple of her glasses near the hinge with her right hand and raising the lens in order to peer through the bifocal as she read. She often called on Jack to decipher the fine print on medication containers, thread needles, and dispense her pills. Climbing the stairs to the house's only bathroom was becoming a challenge.

On May 11, 1985, *The Hamilton Spectator* ran a story about ninety-year-old Jack's military service and his role in the Canadian Legion. "When the Drum Beat Sounded," read the headline, "Jack Was There for His Country."

Later that summer, Alice and Jack spent several weeks with their daughter, Dorothy, and her husband who were then living in North Bay, Ontario. Jack was still surprisingly active and fit. On August 10, he went fishing on Lake Nipissing with his forty-two-year-old grandson, and played soccer on the beach with two of his fifteen-year-old great-grandchildren. Jack showed no signs of slowing down that day. That night, he tucked Alice into bed and promised to kiss her goodnight when he came back from the bathroom. He never returned.

Alice heard a thud and then a commotion in the hallway. She called out to her husband and her daughter.

"Dad's had a fall," came the reply.

Jack died in an instant at 11 p.m. in response to a massive heart attack.

Alice cried, "He promised he'd come back and kiss me goodnight."

After sixty-seven years of marriage, Alice found herself alone and vulnerable. Jack's assistance had become increasingly important to her as her fading eyesight and weakening legs eroded her independence. Their thirty-three descendants and a dozen of their spouses came together to comfort her, but their support could not erase her grief. She maintained her dignity though her anguish was intense, and she missed the man she loved every minute of every day for the remainder of her life.

Jack was buried at White Chapel Gardens in Hamilton on August 15, 1985.

∞∞∞∞∞∞∞∞∞∞∞∞∞∞∞∞∞∞∞∞∞∞∞∞∞∞∞∞∞∞∞∞∞∞

JACK'S LAST DAY

He was a little man, but a ball of fire,
And I am surprised at the weight of his coffin.
Then I realize how many hopes and fears,
And how much courage and pain lie within.

Uneven ground amid tilted bronze markers
Staggers our steps to the distant, gaping, dark hole.
We six descendants, honoured to bear the weight
Of the casket, and the man, and his soul.

The Union Jack trumpets, "Here lies a hero"
A suitable title for the satin-wrapped man.
Through fixed eyes blurred by warm tears of remembrance,
I stare ahead at the gathered black clan.

The priest, in rich garments, the Book in his hands;
The widow, supported by family, shaken,

Await the most ghastly of rituals contrived
To inhume one so suddenly taken.

With putlogs bearing the weight of our burden,
We pallbearers re-join our wives standing alone.
A still moment passes, a bird chirps, and then
The low, mournful birth of a bagpipe's tone.

Tears streaming, hearts aching, we stand through the wail
Of the piper's lament, slow, lingering and sad.
The priest speaking words that all clergy recite.
Rigid, I stare at the piper's gay plaid.

Three decades have passed, and still the grief lingers,
His last day with us forever locked in my mind.
The sadness of losing his presence goes on,
A loss for his kin, a loss for mankind.

∞∞∞∞∞∞∞∞∞∞∞∞∞∞∞∞∞∞∞∞∞∞∞∞∞∞∞∞∞∞∞∞∞∞∞∞

For the most part, Alice's life became uneventful after Jack was gone. She still loved her family and they loved her, but her enthusiasm for life was irrevocably lost. Her daughters shared her care for a while, but the burden became more than they could manage. The little house she had occupied for sixty-seven years was sold, and Alice spent her final days in a nursing home.

Within the first few months after her admission, she was blind, and deaf, and confined to a wheelchair. The home's staff had no idea who she was, what she had experienced, or how she had influenced the world.

On Thursday, 17 November 1988, Alice passed away at Hamilton's General Hospital, at the age of ninety. At the time of her death, she was a Londoner at heart, and yet she was a patriotic Canadian as well. She was the daughter of a maître d', the wife of an adventurer, a mother of five, a grandmother of thirteen and a great-grandmother of twenty-one. She was buried alongside the machine gunner with whom she had fallen in love seventy-two years earlier. During her life, she witnessed two world wars, the reigns of six British monarchs, and a lengthy list of other historic events and inventions.

Alice Geherty was two years old when Queen Victoria died. She was three when the first trans-Atlantic radio transmission reached Europe and five when the Wright brothers made their first powered flight. She was twelve when King George the Fifth was crowned and sixteen when Great Britain went to war with Germany. By the time The war ended, she was a twenty-year-old wife and mother.

At age twenty-one, Alice sailed to Canada where she lived out her life. The Spanish flu killed fifty-million people by the time she celebrated her twenty-second birthday. She was twenty-seven when John Scopes, an American school teacher, was tried for teaching evolution to his students, and twenty-nine when prohibition was repealed in her part of Canada. When the stock market crash of October 1929 triggered the Great Depression, Alice was thirty-one years old.

Two years later, when Al Capone was tried for tax evasion, Alice was thirty-three. She was thirty-nine when Amelia Earhart's plane went missing in the Pacific and forty when the ball-point pen was invented. When World War II began with Germany's invasion of Poland, Alice was forty-one years old. She was forty-three the day Pear Harbour was attacked and forty-seven when the atomic bomb was dropped on Hiroshima. The state of Israel was established a month prior to her fiftieth birthday.

Alice was fifty-two when the Korean War began. When she was fifty-four years of age, television was publicly broadcast in Canada for the first time, and at fifty-five she watched Queen Elizabeth being crowned on a neighbour's TV. Elvis Presley recorded *Hound Dog* when she was fifty-eight.

Alice was sixty-five when John F. Kennedy was assassinated and sixty-seven when the US entered the Vietnam War. She was seventy-one when Neil Armstrong stepped onto the moon. A week before her eighty-second birthday, the first case of AIDS was identified. She was eighty-seven when the Soviet Union's nuclear power plant at Chernobyl suffered a disastrous meltdown and eighty-eight when the first internet domain was registered. When she was eighty-nine, DNA was used to identify a criminal for the first time.

Alice was ninety when she died. Her death marked the end of a life, the end of a generation, and the end of an historic era. Her image, the face of a child in a class photo, the portrait of a young woman on the cover of a book, and the lifeless countenance of a great-grandmother in a satin-lined casket, will fade over time. Those who knew her will cling to their memories of her for a few more years until they too pass away. Then, aside from a few official records bearing her name and the book you have just read, Alice will be forever gone. Still, her impact on those who count her among their ancestors will persist, generation after generation. Understanding, compassion, selflessness and integrity will survive in some of them, in part due to the inspiration of their forgotten ancestor, Alice, who was herself influenced by her ancestors and her beloved husband – the machine gunner.

∞∞∞∞∞∞∞∞∞∞∞∞∞∞∞∞∞∞∞∞∞∞∞∞∞∞∞∞∞∞∞∞∞

REMEMBERING ALICE

Alice came to visit in ninety-eight;
She brought along a loving heart, and strength.
A quiet child, she leaned into her fate.
For others, she would go to any length.

Eighteen, and filled with London sounds and smells,
She met a khaki promise from afar,
Then Alice saw her love endure the Hells
That test the courage of men in time of war.

Mustard gas, and shells, and fear, and worry,
Shared wordless in dark moments during leave.
An infant, then a marriage in a flurry;
By warp and weft of choices did she weave.

Scrawled postcards filled with love from Flanders flew.
The love; the sunshine could not stay the rain;
One day the last man died, and Alice knew
She'd never see her mum and dad again.

At sea aboard a troop-ship, westward bound,
The two endured each passing storm as one,
Called 'Queen' by Mum and Dad though never crowned,
She raised four daughters; mourned a son.

Alice and the Machine Gunner

Grandchildren filled her kitchen, lap and life;
Her values passed to each and every one.
A London child, a mother, and a wife;
In eighty-eight she passed; her story done.

www.ingramcontent.com/pod-product-compliance
Lightning Source LLC
Chambersburg PA
CBHW071435080526
44587CB00014B/1850